Gift 2007

SOUTHEASTERN COMMUNITY
COLLEGE LIBRARY
WHITEVILLE, NC 28472

COMPLIMENTS
of
BEST BOOKS COMPANY

396 Storybook Lane * Chapel Hill, NC 27516 * 1-800-887-4516

JACK WELCH
SPEAKS

Wisdom

from the

World's

Greatest

Business Leader

~ ✷ ~

JACK WELCH SPEAKS

Wisdom

from the

World's

Greatest

Business Leader

JANET C. LOWE

John Wiley & Sons, Inc.

New York • Chichester • Weinheim • Brisbane • Singapore • Toronto

SOUTHEASTERN COMMUNITY
COLLEGE LIBRARY
WHITEVILLE, NC 28472

HD
9697
.A3
U585
1998

This text is printed on acid-free paper.

Copyright © 1998 by Janet C. Lowe. All rights reserved.
Published by John Wiley & Sons, Inc.

Published simultaneously in Canada.

No part of this publication may be reproduced, stored in a retrieval
system or transmitted in any form or by any means, electronic,
mechanical, photocopying, recording, scanning or otherwise, except as
permitted by Section 107 or 108 of the 1976 United States Copyright
Act, without either the prior written permission of the Publisher, or
authorization through payment of the appropriate per-copy fee to the
Copyright Clearance Center, 222 Rosewood Drive, Danvers, MA
01923, (508) 750-8400, fax (508) 750-4744. Requests to the Publisher
for permission should be addressed to the Permissions Department,
John Wiley & Sons, Inc., 605 Third Avenue, New York, NY 10158-
0012, (212) 850-6011, fax (212) 850-6008, E-mail:
PERMREQ@WILEY.COM.

This publication is designed to provide accurate and authoritative
information in regard to the subject matter covered. It is sold
with the understanding that the publisher is not engaged
in rendering legal, accounting, or other professional services.
If legal advice or other expert assistance is required, the services
of a competent professional person should be sought.

Library of Congress Cataloging-in-Publication Data:

Lowe, Janet C.
    Jack Welch speaks : wisdom from the world's greatest
business leader / Janet C. Lowe.
    ISBN 0–471–24272–1

Book design and composition by Anne Scatto/PIXEL PRESS

Printed in the United States of America

10 9 8 7 6 5 4 3

~ ✹ ~

*This book is dedicated
to my dear brothers,
David Walker, Lisle Kincaid,
and Dale Lawrence Lowe.*

~ ✹ ~

CONTENTS

PREFACE

This is a book about leadership, and about one of the most praised and perhaps the most feared, and certainly one of the most confounding and controversial bosses in America. Forget the current buzz that only the Bill Gates-style renegade entrepreneurs effect radical change in business. John Francis "Jack" Welch, chairman and chief executive officer of General Electric Corporation for more than 16 years, has become a global legend, the man who drew the blueprints for the reconstruction of American industry. Three times Welch was voted "most respected CEO" in an *Industry Week* survey of chief executives. In 1995, Welch lost that title to Gates, founder of Microsoft, but only by one vote. *Business Week* proclaimed Welch "the gold standard against which other CEOs are measured."[1]

It hasn't always been so. *Industry Week* also noted that Welch, "the most acclaimed SOB of the last decade (1980s) is the most acclaimed CEO of this one."[2]

When Welch slid behind the wheel at GE in 1981,

he peeled right out onto the road to change—high-speed, gut-wrenching change. Most experts, and certainly many GE employees, couldn't understand why he was ripping up and rebuilding a company that seemed to be in fine shape. Even today, when his company is considered the best managed and one of the most profitable in the world, some critics insist that Welch is engaged in a rapacious drive for size and power.

Let's face it. Jack Welch is not an easy man to like or understand from a distance. Once called the toughest boss in America, Welch has added some of the most feared words to the business lexicon: restructuring, downsizing, rightsizing. He ignited a movement at GE that soon spread to the entire American workforce. But Welch says he isn't a pyromaniac, that he was assigned to the watchtower and told the world he saw smoke. Soon, others saw it too.

When Welch took over at GE, most observers thought he was lucky, stepping into such a successful, well-managed, respected, historic company. A little dull perhaps, but impressive. That year GE's net income was up 9 percent to almost $1.7 billion. Only nine other Fortune 500 companies had earned more. The media, GE's workers, and many others were dumbfounded when Welch urgently demanded change before it was too late.

But Welch had been on the inside for many years. Since graduating from college, he has never worked anywhere but GE. As one observer put it, "Jack

Welch made GE, but GE also made Jack Welch." As an insider, he knew what others had not yet fully recognized: a stodgy GE was headed for ossification. Welch realized that the business world faced cataclysmic changes in its new global, high-technology environment. He also knew GE wasn't ready for it.

Today, however, after nearly two decades of relentless turmoil, GE remains leader of the pack among the best-managed and most financially successful enterprises. Only a handful of U.S. corporations of GE's age remain at the forefront of their industries and are formidable competitors in the global arena. "Welch's GE," says Victor H. Vroom, a professor at the Yale School of Organization and Management, "is a model for the promise—and the problems—of creating the modern industrial company."[3]

Despite his critics, many management experts think of Welch as a "tough-love capitalist." He did these things, they say, for the good of GE and, ultimately, the well-being of the entire country. In time, other corporate leaders were forced to follow his lead and gird their companies for technology-driven, globe-trotting competition.

Who is this feared and admired top executive? If, as Welch claims, the label toughest boss in America is unfair, the toughest competitor in America is not. GE employees may quake when they get a call from Welch, but CEOs of competitor companies dread a GE wake-up call even more.

The Economist described him as a "restless Irish-

American."[4] That description doesn't apply if restless means a person who can't settle, and moves merely to keep moving. It is accurate if it characterizes someone who never seems to rest. An outgoing, exuberant news and information junkie, Welch speaks with a slight stammer, bites his nails, and looks every minute his age. Though his fringe of hair is gray, Welch's 5'8" frame is trim and wiry. His penetrating, pale-blue eyes sparkle with curiosity, interest, and intellect.

The year after he was appointed head of GE, *The Wall Street Journal* reported, "Mr. Welch can spend a day visiting a factory, jump on a plane, catch a few hours sleep, and start all over again; in between, he might stop in Sun Valley, Idaho, and as he puts it, 'ski like crazy for five days.'"[5]

It's apparent he still has fire in the belly at age 62 when he speaks. Welch spikes words across sentences like a volleyball player smashing a ball over the net. He slams his points home like a bridge player holding all the high cards in the trump suit. He speaks in short, incomplete sentences, marked by the accent of a Boston cop. He is famous for interrupting subordinates when they hesitate momentarily. He is sometimes "excitable to excess," former GE vice chairman Edward Hood once conceded.[6]

Even ill health didn't slow down Welch. In May 1995, he underwent quintuple bypass heart surgery. He returned to work on Labor Day, 1995. Within 12 months, he seemed fitter than ever, and told reporters, "I feel great."[7]

The Washington Post once called Welch an "unlikely prophet," yet despite its stuffy reputation, GE has long been dedicated to management innovation. Notions such as strategic planning, decentralization, and market research all arose from the fertile brains of GE managers. It is no surprise, then, that sound management flows from GE culture, a company that promises to bring "good things to life." But few people expected the originality and daring that Welch brought to the job.

Indeed, Welch did not follow a traditional career path at the company. He started out in a plastics skunk works, and deftly sidestepped the corporate mainstream for most of his work life. Welch entered the race for GE's top slot perceived as an outsider, too young and too troublesome. Welch got the job in his own way, and he does the job his own way.

He realizes that as chairman of GE he is always on stage, that his words, actions, and even his body language are being interpreted worldwide. Ironically, Welch would prefer not to have too much public attention.

When Ralph Nader and William Taylor wrote a book called *The Big Boys: Power & Position in American Business*, they attempted to interview Welch.

Welch demurred at our interview request when he was approached in March 1984. He argued that he had a "short tenure as CEO"—he had assumed the helm at GE three years earlier—although he did give us a rain check. In a telephone call to him several months later, I received a more animated reaction. I was making a final entreaty for an interview when suddenly Welch's voice changed to a mixture of rapid pleading and a "lemme outta here" tone. "I don't need this," he cried. "I'm just a boy with knickers and a lollipop. I don't want to be part of a book. I'm just a grungy, lousy manager...You can have access to the company on any other basis...I don't want a high profile.... I'm just a grunt. .... I'm just a man in a room." No combination of written words could capture the wonderfully off-the-cuff, ingenuous voice of this supercharged general of GE.[8]

When I requested an interview, Welch at first refused, sending a handwritten note saying that he had no interest in a book about himself. Joyce Hergenhan, vice president for public relations, intercepted the second request and intervened. She persuaded Welch to meet with me, but even then he was reluctant. At the end of a 90-minute interview, he had softened a bit. "I still wish you weren't doing this, but I do feel a *little* better now that I've met you."

~

This is my second book about a business leader, primarily stated in his own words. The first was the bestseller, *Warren Buffett Speaks*. Though Buffett and Welch are vastly different men with different styles, skills, goals, and accomplishments, there are similarities between the two. Both are the absolute best at what they do. Both are intensely smitten with their work and focused on it. Both men are out-front, unabashedly American middle class. Both attended public school and graduated from state universities. Buffett was raised a Protestant and Welch is Catholic, and though neither seems to attend church often as adults, both bring bedrock moral and ethical standards to their jobs. In the same way that Buffett led the Midwest to triumph over Wall Street, Welch led factory town-New England to victory over international business. Both show us that the American dream survives. They both demonstrate that everyday people have plenty of dignity, capability, and intelligence to accomplish whatever they aspire to do.

Buffett and Welch have another experience in common. They both were bitten by Wall Street, Welch when GE acquired Kidder Peabody, and Buffett when he invested in Salomon Brothers. But more about Welch's experience in the book ahead.

One last similarity: Both men share their ideas liberally. Buffett's Berkshire Hathaway annual report has become a best-seller among professional and individual investors. *The Washington Post* says that Welch's "annual letter to shareholders has become closely watched by other corporate leaders and business professors for news on the latest thinking on management, and his techniques are being adopted throughout corporate America." [9]

Of course Welch has blemishes and blind spots. One of them became apparent during our interview. Whenever I asked Welch a question, he invariably directed his answer to my husband, a retired aerospace executive, who came along to monitor the tape recorder. Later in the interview, when discussing the importance of diversity, Welch said that GE is striving very hard to make sure that African Americans are represented at all levels of the company. "The advancement of women has taken care of itself," he added. Though women do hold some high level positions at GE, it's hard to believe that sex-based barriers have been totally eliminated in such a large corporation.

Some observers claim that Welch's great contribution to GE has been the matching of technology and markets. Others say it is his role as a change agent. Certainly, he truly Americanized GE—bringing the democratic process, the voice of the ordinary worker, into the corporate arena—while at the same time pushing GE into global leadership.

Experts point out—and Welch himself claims—that not all of his ideas are original. They spring from many sources. His skill has been the ability to recognize good ideas, distill them, and implement them in a company with as many workers as Akron, Ohio, has residents, and with revenues larger than the gross domestic products of approximately half the nations of the world.

∿

A few words of guidance to the reader. Because this book is composed mainly of Welch's comments, it paints a picture of the GE that Welch hopes and aims for, not necessarily the GE that others see, or even the GE that is. At times, it is difficult to separate Jack Welch from the company he heads, but readers should remind themselves to do so. I've tried to make that distinction clear.

It may seem that this book canonizes Jack Welch, although I've tried to avoid that impression. Clearly, he would not have been chosen as a topic unless I believed there was much to learn from him. Even so, the goal is to capture the whole person, to understand who he is, and how and why he does what he does. I believe that if you listen to people talk about almost any subject, they reveal a great deal about themselves in the process. Listen to the words Welch uses most frequently: game, compete, speed, performance, and winning. In fact, winning seems to be almost a spiritual concept with Welch, right up there with enlightenment or grace. It's also encouraging to notice how often Welch uses the words freedom, truth, quality, and love.

He has the habit, in his speeches and writings, of issuing warnings to individuals or business enterprises who may be in danger of extinction. GE employees have become as adept as State Department diplomats at interpreting his words. For example, in an interview published in GE's house organ, *Monogram*, the writer asked whether Welch had any new ideas to communicate. He replied: "You're right about how highly I value communications. . . . But the more I understand the subject, I think perhaps we've all focused a bit too much on techniques, like choosing to use this publication or making another videotape. Certainly, the medium's important, and while just about all our businesses have done an outstanding job in providing good, candid information on competitors, on customers, on markets—we've got to go beyond that."[10]

Not long after that, the publication was gone— discontinued.

Welch often explains that the business world is riddled with paradoxes, and that successful leaders in the future will accept paradox as normal. Well, Jack Welch is a paradox himself, and says Dr. Steve Kerr, GE's chief learning officer, that is the most interesting thing about the man. His complexity makes him unique, sometimes exasperating, but always intriguing.

Remember, too, while reading this book, that Welch's comments were not made in the order that they appear here. They have been grouped together by topics or by ideas that allow Welch's life and personality to unfold. Refer to the footnotes for details on where and when he made a particular comment. A time line is included in case the reader wants to check the progression of events.

~

In 1988, just seven years after Welch took charge at GE, the *Financial Times*, a British newspaper, posed questions about Welch that people everywhere were asking:

> What is it really like inside the new GE? Has its traditional ability to develop and sustain long-term strategies been replaced completely by a process which fosters only naked opportunism and flight from the Japanese, as Welch's many critics claim—especially since last year's sale of the $3 billion GE-RCA consumer electronics business?
>
> Or has he, true to GE's long tradition of pioneering management techniques, found an unusually effective way of running a giant, $39 billion corporation, almost as if he were an entrepreneur in charge of a set of recent start-ups? If his approach does work, can it outlast him? And what are the implications for other companies, both large and medium-sized, which have copied the old GE model, or are still just starting to do so? [11]

The answer to at least one of those questions appeared in *Business Week* a year earlier: "Like him or not, Jack Welch has succeeded in sweeping a major American company clean of the bureaucratic excesses of the past and transforming a paternalistic culture into one that puts winning in the marketplace above all other concerns. Like it or not, the management styles of more U.S. companies are going to look a lot more like GE."[12]

I've tried to address the rest of the questions in this book. Ultimately, readers must decide for themselves what they think about America's most visible and relentless agent for change.

Welch politely—and sincerely—ends most of his speeches with the same comment, "Thanks for listening." I end this introduction with a similar sentiment. Thanks for reading.

Janet Lowe

August 1, 1997

ACKNOWLEDGMENTS

Thanks to my editor at John Wiley & Sons, Inc., Myles Thompson, along with Jennifer Pincott, Robin Goldstein, Laurie Thompson, and others at Wiley for their enthusiasm, support, and expert knowledge.

Many thanks to my literary agent Alice Fried Martell, for her faith and diligence. Joyce Hergenham and Dr. Steve Kerr of General Electric were extremely helpful in preparing this book. Support for the book also was provided by Art and Lorena Goeller, Randall Michler, Barbara Yagerman, and Bill Bryant. And much appreciation to my husband, Austin Lynas, for his patience and hard work.

IN ONE DECADE:
FROM LETTERMAN
TO SEINFELD

"I love Seinfeld. I think it's sensational television. It somehow hits every bone I've got. I wouldn't chase any other program."[13]

Welch has plenty of reasons to adore the trendy NBC television sitcom. *Seinfeld* was the most successful television series of all time. It was the first to command more than $1 million a minute for advertising—a distinction previously limited to the Super Bowl. Not only is *Seinfeld* wildly popular, its vast viewership has enabled NBC, a General Electric subsidiary, to slot shows around it on the schedule to maximize their popularity. In 1997, NBC dominated prime time television, plus morning, evening, and late-night news ratings.

Ratings, naturally, lead to higher advertising rates and higher profits. In 1996, NBC made seven times more money than ABC, the only other network to be profitable. NBC profits, plus another $500 million kicked in by cable and television station operations, added up to nearly $1 billion in GE's operating profits that year. *Seinfeld* contributed $200 million a year to those profits.

NBC, home to the *Milton Berle Show*, *Bonanza*, *Cheers*, and dozens of other classics, has proved its ability to present memorable television programming. Yet despite the track record, *Seinfeld*'s popularity and NBC's profitability were rousing personal victories for Jack Welch. The NBC saga is the Jack Welch story in a nutshell.

When he announced, in December 1985, that GE would buy RCA (NBC's parent company) for $6.3 billion in cash, Welch was euphoric. Not only was it the largest corporate acquisition up to that time, the deal brought a lost child home. GE founded RCA in 1919, shortly after buying the rights to Guglielmo Marconi's radio technology. In 1933, to the great disappointment of company executives, the threat of antitrust litigation forced GE to sell the subsidiary.

"Welch foresees no indigestion from swallowing RCA," wrote *Newsweek*. "He will continue to run RCA with the hands-off supervision that is the essence of his management style. Speaking of the NBC Chairman Grant Tinker and his team, he says, 'They're our type of people. They know how to be number 1 and we know how to give people who know how to be number 1 money.'" [14]

Not only was RCA a golden asset, "The network business acts as a counterbalance to more cyclical manufacturing businesses," Welch explained. [15]

But it wasn't long before NBC and GE were locked in one of the most publicized culture clashes of all time. There was an instant and acid reaction to the acquisition from NBC late-night talk show hosts, especially David Letterman, who, among other things, called GE's management "knuckleheads."

Right after the announcement came, Letterman hauled a camera crew to the old GE building in New York City. "You never know what you're in for when you get a brand-new boss. So when General Electric bought the company, RCA and NBC, I thought I would drop by the GE building here in midtown Manhattan, meet my new employers, kind of, you know, get things off on the right foot." The videotape showed Letterman ambling down Lexington Avenue, a basket of fruit clutched in both hands: "Sometime in August, I guess, the takeover will be complete, and we're all getting a little curious as to what kind of effect it's going to have on NBC as we know it today—the program and, I guess, specifically, how is it going to influence me? And what I'm really trying to get at here is, am I going to have a job? So this is the General Electric building, and I have a little gift, and we thought: What the heck? Let's just drop in and say hello, just see how it's going. They can't object to that, can they?"

At the door of GE headquarters, a voice blasted from a speaker: "This is not a building to film in. Clear the front of the GE building please." A woman stepped out of the revolving door with a security guard at her side. "I'm not sure you're able to do this. We haven't gotten any authorization." "You mean we need authorization to drop off a fruit basket? Oh this is going to be fun to work with these people, isn't it? To drop off a fruit basket you need paperwork," Letterman chided.

Letterman politely persisted his way into the building where the security guard demanded that the cameras be turned off. Letterman agreed, then reached out to shake the security guard's hand. The guard reached out, but thought again and pulled his hand away at the last minute, jabbing his thumb in the air. "Shut off the camera please." Finally, the guard put his hand over the camera's lens.

The "security gentleman" became a star on Letterman's show. "Maybe you didn't realize that we got to see a glimpse of the official General Electric handshake," Letterman hooted. Then he showed the hand-out/thumb-up gesture over and over again as the audience rolled in laughter.

Welch says he wasn't upset. The video was shown in the GE boardroom and at GE's training facility at Crotonville. "It was fun" (Welch laughed). "From then on we'd tease the guard when we went in the building—give him the GE handshake."[16]

But Letterman wouldn't let it go, cracking that the head of GE's small appliance division would push for a miniseries on the development of the toaster oven. When asked by a student at Harvard Business School if he minded David Letterman frequently calling GE executives "pinheads," Welch said he didn't care, as long as Letterman's ratings kept rising.[17]

Soon, however, NBC did feel heat from GE. Though NBC dominated prime time, plus morning, evening, and late-night news ratings, Welch thought they could be more profitable, especially the money-bleeding news operation. In 1987, NBC news was losing $150 million annually, which Welch thought unnecessary.

Because of their important role as part of the fourth estate of democracy, news executives felt their first responsibility was to produce excellent programs. The entertainment arm, always profitable, could pick up the slack. Some members of the news operation were insulted that Welch didn't put their business on a higher moral plane than other GE businesses.

Welch however believed that all of GE's products, everything from lightbulbs to refrigerators, carried the responsibility of public trust: "Every GE engine attached to a plane, people bet their lives with. That's a public trust and greater in many ways than a network."[18]

Laying off hundreds of GE turbine employees, Welch said, was no worse than cutbacks in TV news. News may be responsible for informing the public, but turbine workers were important, too. They, in fact, were at a disadvantage: "They have no press to write about them," Welch claimed.[19]

Welch was particularly irritated when NBC paid $300 million for the rights to broadcast the 1988

Seoul Olympics, but attracted only a 30 percent share. Welch contended NBC's Olympic presentation was dull: "They are running a semi-news operation rather than a heroic sports event," Welch complained "It's as if the shuttle went up and they were talking about Franco-American relations."[20]

Grant Tinker, who made NBC number one and who left even though Welch wanted him to stay, explained the change that had occurred: "My idea of running NBC was to get it up to top speed, make a lot of money; and so we spilled a little, who cares? To the extent it becomes just a maximize-the-bottom line kind of company, some of the air will go out of NBC."[21]

Differences between GE and NBC flared on other fronts.

* When NBC's headquarters at 30 Rockefeller Plaza in New York City were remodeled, employees wanted to replace the large RCA on the building with the network initials. Welch reinforced the relationship between the network and the company by insisting that the GE "meatball," the intertwined G and E, replace the historic RCA logo.

* GE dumped its Miami affiliate, WSVN-TV, and replaced it with WTVJ-TV, previously a CBS affiliate. It was the first time a network had acquired a station aligned with a rival network. GE paid an eye-popping $270 million to do so.

At NBC's 1987 management conference in Fort Lauderdale, Welch painted his vision of GE and NBC's place within. He asked the question, "Was NBC better off under RCA or GE?" then answered it himself: "I'd say for the good people, it's a dynamite deal. For the turkeys, it's only marginal."[22]

Welch then chilled the audience by suggesting that the turkeys didn't have much of a future at GE and shouldn't hang around.

> *"We're going to demand from you earnings growth every year. And don't give us any shrugs about that. Those are the rules of the road.... You take charge of your destiny. If you don't, we will."*[23]

Welch assured executives that he loved NBC; furthermore, if the network kept its ratings high, GE could push past Exxon to rival IBM for the company with the largest market evaluation in the world. "And the more value this company has, the more things we can buy," Welch said. [24]

GE and NBC were slam-dancing by now.

"These guys (Welch and his appointed NBC chief Robert Wright) have no commitment to the business they're in," said Larry Grossman, former president of NBC news. "They buy and sell companies. GE is a venture capital company. That's what makes the light shine in Jack's and Bob's [Wright] eyes.... There's no commitment to people or product." [25]

But not everyone was offended by Welch's remarks at the Fort Lauderdale conference. "I wasn't intimidated; I was inspired," said Warren Littlefield, who apparently grasped Welch's full message. Littlefield later became president, then chairman of NBC Entertainment.[26]

Oddly, while network executives and the NBC news organization struggled with Welch's ideology, NBC's California entertainment contingency seemed happier.

Michele Brusten, head of NBC's comedy production unit, said: "None of us liked RCA. We were like children to them." GE, on the other hand, respected and encouraged the creativity, debate, and free flow of ideas from Hollywood.[27]

Heads rolled and management changed at NBC. David Letterman, after he was passed over as Johnny Carson's successor, moved to CBS. NBC's *Tonight Show with Jay Leno* became the leader among late-night talk shows.

Despite the tighter budgets and higher financial goals, in 1989 NBC set records, boasting 68 consecutive weeks as the top-rated TV network.

Even after NBC management accepted the notion that it must maximize efficiency as much as possible, the heat wasn't off. At a subsequent management conference, Welch was pressed with the question: When will it—the pressure to be more profitable—end? "In the world of the '80s and the '90s it won't end," Welch replied.[28]

~

Wounds healed slowly. In 1992, NBC employees still hadn't recovered from the shock of meeting Jack Welch face to face. One executive told *Working Woman* magazine: "Most people here would either prefer to be back in the days before GE or to be working for another company."[29]

But by 1997, when NBC paid more for *Seinfeld*—$120 million—than had ever been paid for a TV show, NBC was the undisputed leader in all segments of network TV. Quality remained high and profits blazed. *Fortune* wrote that Robert C. Wright, Welch's so-called know-nothing lawyer picked to run the network, had turned it into a "powerhouse TV business."[30]

Comedian Jerry Seinfeld, star of the show, decided to call it quits at the end of the 1997–1998 season. He wanted to bow out while the show was still a hit.

By then, NBC was a core in GE's information business, and 1997 its most profitable year ever. The message? Good management practices apply to any business. You can be both excellent and profitable. In fact, the only hope for long-term survival is to be both.

Welch was right on another count. The pressure didn't end. In the mid-1990s, television viewing overall was on the decline, and even that viewership was split between a growing number of new networks and a vast range of cable programs.

By the summer of 1997, all the networks were cutting costs and laying off people. "The future is going to be very different," said John Eck, NBC's newly appointed quality officer. "This is all about survival."[31]

For Welch, the realignment of attitudes at NBC was just part of his job.

"People say, 'Jack, how can you be at NBC; you don't know anything about dramas or comedies . . .'" Welch explained. *"Well, I can't build a jet engine, either. I can't build a turbine. Our job at GE is to deal with resources—human and financial. The idea of getting great talent, giving them all the support in the world, and letting them run is the whole management philosophy of GE, whether it's in turbines, engines, or a network."[32]*

AN AMERICAN ODYSSEY

GROWING UP IN SALEM

Ask Jack Welch where he was born and he'll say "Pibiddy," pronouncing Peabody the Massachusetts way. Jack grew up in the next town over, Salem, in a middle-class neighborhood filled with big old houses and tall trees, and bounded on three sides by cemeteries.

Number 15 Locust Street is a two-story frame house, not large but not small, surrounded by towering oaks and elms. Today, a "senior citizen crossing" sign marks the end of the lane. "My cousin lives next door. One family on the corner, the St. Pierre's, had seven children, and I think three or four of them still live in the area. All those years. People take pretty good care of their property there," Welch says.[33]

Even in a town famous for seventeenth century witch trials and other spooky stories, young Jack wasn't bothered much by the ghostly neighbors.

"My parents were so cute: My father always told me a cemetery was the best neighbor you could have. It's

quiet, it doesn't yell at you. Of course, I bought that.
I thought that was the way it was."34

Welch's family was what Americans call middle class and what the British call working class. The Welches were neither poor nor affluent. His father worked for the Boston & Maine Railroad, and his mother stayed home with Jack. The family could afford a summer home. Because he was an only child, Welch says, he was loved, nurtured, and praised more than many children.

"My parents were about 40 when they had me, and they had been trying for 16 years. My father was a railroad conductor, a good man, hardworking, passive. He went to work at 5 A.M., got home at 7:30 at night. My mother and I would drive down to the train station in Salem, Massachusetts, to pick him up. Often, the train would be late, so we'd sit for hours and talk. I was very close to her. She was a dominant mother. She always felt I could do anything. It was my mother who trained me, taught me the facts of life. She wanted me to be independent. Control your own destiny—she always had that idea. Saw reality. No mincing words. Whenever I got out of line, she would whack me one. But always positive. Always constructive. Always uplifting. And I was just nuts about her."35

"Don't get me started on my mother. She's my whole game."36

Grace Welch always expressed her confidence in Jack's abilities.

> "*She told me I didn't have a speech impediment,*" referring to his stutter. "*Just that my brain worked too fast.*"[37]

Welch may have inherited several characteristics from his mother:

> "*If you came to her house and said you liked her glasses, she gave them to you. She did taxes for people in the neighborhood. She was very quick with numbers. If somebody crossed her, I remember her remembering that. She was loyal to friends, and strong against those she felt wronged her.*"[38]

Welch says his mother taught him three important lessons: to communicate candidly, to face reality, and to control your own destiny.

Grace Welch died in 1966, and Jack Welch says at that time, though he'd been devoutly religious before, his interest in Catholicism waned.

~

As a youngster, Jack often played in "the pit," an abandoned quarry where the neighborhood boys gathered for impromptu baseball and basketball games. It was a rough-and-tumble place where Welch won a reputation for taking charge, often organizing the matches. It was on the playground, Welch says, where his leadership skills took root.

"It's a series of reinforcing confidence builders that we all go through. When you're elected captain of the team, when you are in the playground picking teams, you sort of grab one team; it just happens— you're used to a series of experiences, and people look to you and respond favorably to you."[39]

One of those granite-pit friends, Lawrence McIntyre, became superintendent of parks and recreation in Salem. He agrees with Welch. "There is a group of about 15 guys who made out pretty well. A lot of us didn't go to college. We just worked hard and ended up with positions. Jack and all of us grew up in that very competitive atmosphere, so when we went out into the world, we said, 'Hey, we can do anything. Nothing can be as tough as going to the pit.'"[40]

At Salem High School, Welch loved hockey. When he was at the lowest point of his popularity at GE, his hockey background provided fodder for gossip. Employees swapped stories that Welch spent more time in the penalty box than anyone else on his high school team. "That's just crazy," says Welch. "I don't know where that came from. That is the last thing. I was a little stick handler; you can see by my size. I wasn't that big. I was not whacking guys. I was the center. The center doesn't get a lot of penalties in hockey. Defensemen do."

"When this game gets going, there are enough inventions out there about yourself. It happens all the time. The stories are insane, insane.*"[41]*

Welch may not have been whacking guys, but he was playing the game at full power. Samuel Zoll, a childhood friend of Welch's recalls: "He was a nice, regular guy, but always very competitive, relentless, and argumentative."[42]

Even as a teen, Welch must have realized he was brash. Welch's high school magazine lists his favorite saying as, "Are we still pals?"[43]

For someone who grew up in a town that capitalizes on its history, Welch doesn't spend much time on nostalgia. In 1994, Welch was asked about his retirement plans, and his reply described his orientation to time:

> *"When I stop learning something new and start talking about the past versus the future, I will go."*[44]

Welch recalls his childhood fondly and says that his life has been easy.

THE FIRST TO GO TO COLLEGE

Welch's mother was devoutly religious and Jack was an altar boy at St. Thomas the Apostle Church, but he didn't go to parochial school; Jack attended Pickering Elementary, a public school within walking distance of his home, then went on to the big, brick Salem Classical High School.

There he lettered in hockey, and though his team became league champions, it wasn't always on top. In Welch's junior year, the Salem High School yearbook,

The Witch, reported that the team didn't make the playoffs. However, "the team came to life at the end of the season by beating their archrival, Beverly, 1-0."

Welch was voted "most talkative and noisiest boy" in his class, and the high school literary magazine listed as Jack's repressed desire "to make a million."[45]

Welch and two other friends from Salem High were nominated for Navy ROTC college scholarships, which would provide full room, board, and tuition. Welch was disappointed when his friends received the scholarships but he did not. "I don't know what my problem was. I didn't know enough people. I can remember my father calling our congressman and things like that. He didn't really know how to do it very well," Welch said.[46]

Though the University of Massachusetts did not have the prestige of nearby Amherst and Smith Colleges, it has many distinguished graduates, including Jack Smith, chairman of General Motors. And the spartan UMass campus, which sits like an old New England mill town in the midst of rolling green hills, was fertile soil for Jack Welch.

"If I'd gone to the Massachusetts Institute of Technology I would have been down at the bottom of the pile and never got my head out. By going to a small state school I was fortunate enough to get a lot of self-confidence. See, I'm a firm believer that all of these experiences build these self-confidences in you: your mother's knee, playing sports, going to

school, getting grades. I had some kids in my high school who did better than I did, so instead of going to UMass, they went to MIT. And they ended up in the middle of the pack among some of the brightest kids in the country. And didn't get the confidence, and the reinforcing. I mean I was a golden boy in chemical engineering at UMass, with very nice teachers, good people."[47]

~

"UMass gave me a lot of breaks because I was the first person in my family to go to college. I literally had no idea what I wanted to be. I had an uncle who was an engineer at a power station in Salem, so an engineer was something. I took chemistry and fell in love with chemistry. And chemistry and engineering went together."[48]

"I wanted to do well. I wanted to get a degree. But I didn't know what was going to happen."[49]

Neither did his mother. Grace Welch had the traditional dreams—she would have liked her son to be a priest or a doctor.

~

In his sophomore year Welch pledged Phi Sigma Kappa and moved into a fraternity house by the campus pond. "I was the only engineer, or one of very few in the place. Most were football players," Welch recalled.[50]

"We were on scholastic ban all the time. We drank more beer and had more fights than anybody there. And we'd play cards all night, and I had great grades."[51]

Welch was on the dean's list all four years and did honors work as a senior. His professors encouraged him to go to graduate school and helped him apply for fellowships. Though Welch attributes this to luck, the picture in his college yearbook shows a young man shining with promise. Welch's clean-cut face nearly leaps off the page, so filled is it with earnest enthusiasm.

William Mahoney, a Massachusetts businessman who was president of Welch's class at UMass, also saw the early signs of success: "It was in his eyes. He was always looking one step ahead. He hated losing, even in touch football," Mahoney said.[52]

"All of my professors—many of them have died now—were my friends until the day they died. I was sort of like their child. They pushed me through. Professors Richardson and Ernie Lindsey, who was the head of the chemical engineering department. They just liked me and they took care of me, boosted me."[53]

"Then I went to graduate school because I got good grades in college. A professor said, 'you should go to graduate school.' I got a bunch of fellowships, and I decided I'd go there. . . . I went to (the University of)

Illinois, which had a great reputation in engineer-
ing, and I had a lot of places to go because I was in
the top of the class at a school that wasn't MIT, so it
was easier to shine in this pond."

～

Welch met Carolyn Osburn at Lenten mass while at
the University of Illinios. They married in 1959 and
had two sons and two daughters. Jack and Carolyn
were divorced, apparently amicably, in 1985, and both
have since remarried.

～

Welch says he left grad school with one career goal:

"I wanted to make $30,000 by the time I was 30."54

SPORTS WERE EVERYTHING

Jack Welch grew up playing endless games of baseball, basketball, and hockey, either in the streets of
Salem or in an abandoned gravel pit near his home.

"We were all jocks of sorts. I mean, we played ball
countless hours, played street hockey all night. That
was everything. Sports were everything."55

～

Welch's parents often carted him off to Fenway Park,
where they sat in the bleachers and watched the Red
Sox play baseball. He became a walking encyclopedia
on the team.

Welch first met Joyce Hergenhan, Con Edison's senior vice president for public affairs when, over dinner, he interviewed her for a position at GE. Knowing that she, too, was a sports fan, Welch asked:

"Who played second base for the 1946 Red Sox?"

"Bobby Doerr," she replied.

"Yeah, but who held the ball?" asked Welch.

"Oh, you mean when Enos Slaughter scored from first base on a single?"

"What else would I mean?" Welch growled.

"Johnny Pesky!" shot back Hergenhan. [56]

Hergenhan was one of the first employees that Welch hired on becoming CEO, and she is on GE's corporate executive council.

～

To say that Welch is passionate about sports is an understatement. He is seen at such fashionable events as the French Open tennis tournament and the Kentucky Derby. But mostly, he tromps off to the best golf courses. He played with President Bill Clinton during the president's 1997 vacation on Nantucket. Welch also golfs at the Augusta National, where he is a member.

～

Welch plays as aggressively as he works. He once skied for an entire day with a dislocated knee. A former college roommate remembers Welch as a fearsome competitor with average skills: "Jack wasn't blessed with a lot of grace or athletic ability. He trounced people by trying harder."[57]

Welch admits as much:

> *"My hockey was good in high school, but I never got any better. It was really funny, in the 8th and 9th grades . . . I was the best pitcher in Salem. I was pitching against seniors, but then by the time I was a senior I was on the bench, because I never got any faster. I had a clever curve ball, and all that stuff. Same thing in college. In high school, I was on the all-star hockey team. In college? I couldn't skate fast enough. I topped out in sports so early, except for golf."[58]*

The Welches live near the Fairfield Country Club and have a second home on Nantucket, both of which allow them to indulge in their passion for golf. "My game is at a whole new level," Welch says.

After playing golf most of his life, suddenly Welch was playing with a 6 handicap. A year after open-heart surgery, he broke 70 for the first time. But he says it wasn't the surgery that made the difference.

> *"It was the second marriage that took my golf game to a whole new level. Because my wife was a lawyer in New York, and one of the first weekends we went away together, I went out and played golf. She looked at me like—she got the weekend off and I went out and played golf? I'd done that all my life and I*

didn't know any better. She said, 'Wait a minute. This isn't the way it's going to be.' And so she said, 'I've got to learn to play golf with you. You've got to teach me how to play golf.' So I did, and she's now a single-digit handicapper. In eight years. By teaching her, I focused on golf in a way that I'd never done. And I've gone to a whole new level. It's amazing, isn't it?"[59]

Walter Wriston, the former CEO of Citicorp, and his wife, Kathy, introduced Welch to his second wife, Jane Beasly, a former mergers and acquisitions lawyer. They were married in 1989. And, Welch hastens to point out, "I've got a great marriage."[60]

∼

Science also is having an influence on Welch's game:

"I think what is happening in golf, frankly, is that the technology is going on this curve, and the aging process is going on this curve, and the technology is outpacing the aging. The club is getting bigger, wider."

∼

"I use the biggest Big Bertha. Ely Callaway has been very generous to me. He has been giving me clubs—because we own half of Callaway through a silly investment GE made. But it worked out. Ely Callaway's been a wonderful friend. He just sent me a new driver [with which] I can hit a mile."

"Everyone's golf game's getting better. We're play-ing at levels we're all stunned by. Places we never thought we'd be. The technology's moved tremen-dously. It's very curious to see technology outpacing age."[61]

ICE CAN'T FORM ON
A SWIFT-MOVING STREAM

In the classic 1967 film *The Graduate*, a family friend offered career advice to young Dustin Hoffman. "Plastics," he whispered in Hoffman's ear. Welch got the point, and by no means did he consider the advice vacuous. By 1967, Welch was a rising young executive at General Electric's plastics division.

When he graduated from the University of Illinois in 1960 with a Ph.D. in chemical engineering, Welch got three job offers. He chose GE. "It was in Massa-chusetts, where I came from, so it was like going home in a way. That may sound ridiculous, but in those days that was kind of important."[62]

Welch and his first bride loaded up the brand new Volkswagen Beetle that his father had given him as a graduation gift and drove to Pittsfield, 160 miles from his hometown. There he started his first full-time job earning $10,500 per year.

Welch started in a GE skunk works with one lab assistant, but soon was running a little operation that helped introduce a whole new material into society. Competing with the likes of Dow Chemical and Du-

Pont, Welch helped vault GE Plastics from a $28 million sideline to a billion-dollar business.

~

Welch relished the free-wheeling atmosphere at the R&D facility:

> *"In the very early days of plastics, we were brash—excited; brilliant on some days, dumb on others, but we were never arrogant because we couldn't afford to be—with customers, suppliers, with each other."*[63]

There were problems with the color and malleability of the formula he'd been assigned, but Welch buckled down to solve them. He made rapid progress, but at the end of his first year, GE granted him only the standard $1,000 raise. The explanation? Everyone got the same raise, good performers and bad. Disgusted, Welch quit and took a chemical engineering job at International Minerals & Chemicals in Chicago. Just days before he was to start, Ruben Gutoff, a GE vice president, lured him back with more responsibility and a higher salary. "Somebody told me they loved me." Welch said.[64]

~

In 1968, Welch became GE's youngest general manager. He was 33 years old, and the head of a department that produced and marketed the plastics Lexan and Noryl. There was little use for plastics until Welch started showing the makers of baby bottles, automobiles, and small appliances how much cheaper, lighter, and more durable his plastics would be than the material they were using. He went after every possible market, even persuading a researcher to clad a GE toaster in plastic. His group developed a television advertisement showing a bull charging through a china shop. Everything shattered, except the dishes made of Lexan. The ploy worked. Plastics became so commonplace on everything from automobiles to appliances to footwear that most consumers now don't give it a second thought.

~

"I was lucky enough to join GE in a place where I was, like, the only employee. So I hired my first technician. I was emperor, king, prince—you pick the title, okay? I took my employee home with me. Introduced him to my family. He knew my kids. We started a pilot plant, and when we got a little more money, we hired two, and three, and then four. So it was a rare break. Starting with a piece of chemistry, and saying, 'Go make something out of this Jack.' I remember going down to the hardware store, buying this stuff to put the kettles together, my technician and I. People talk about communication across layers—that's all we had. The two of us. We communicated. We called it a family grocery store. We were all friends. As I went to bigger pieces of GE, I found bigger bureaucracies—layers and all that stuff—and it wasn't friendly. Business was very

serious—turf—boxes. Business isn't that. Business is ideas and fun and excitement and celebrations, all those things."[65]

～

"Some of the most exciting and memorable times of my life will always be those frantic days as part of a team trying to grow a plastics business out of Pittsfield. Bureaucracy simply cannot get a foothold in an environment like that, the way ice can't form in a fast-moving stream."[66]

～

At age 37, Welch became group executive for the $1.5 billion components and materials group. This included all of plastics, plus GE medical systems. Though other group executives moved to the new corporate headquarters in Fairfield, Connecticut, Welch demurred:

"I stayed in Pittsfield Mass., through all kinds of promotions. Myself and an older fellow, Gerhardt Neumann; he ran our engines business; [he was] a legendary German figure. He stayed in his business. The other group executives all came to Fairfield in '74 when they moved here. Again, I had the support of a vice chairman named Herm Weiss, who was a cover story for Sports Illustrated's *25th anniversary, as a great athlete/businessman. I came down [to headquarters] and asked if I could stay in Pittsfield, and he let me. And Reg Jones got so mad. He said,*

'You . . . how could you ask him.? *I was the one you should have asked.' I had my kids and I didn't want to move them. I ran a large group out of a hotel in Pittsfield.*"[67]

~

Welch installed a special telephone in his office. All the purchasing agents in his group had the number and if a buyer won a price concession from a vendor, he could call and share the good news. Welch immediately congratulated the agent on shaving a few cents off the price of steel, or whatever he had done. Welch then followed up with a personal thank-you note.

It was a formative time for Welch, who says that everyone should work in a fast-growing business like plastics or financial services:

"GE trained with good businesses and bad ones. I always felt sorry for the people in the bad ones because they never saw a good one. All they really did was work in the vineyard they were sent to toil in. They always compared themselves with their direct competitor. So if their returns were nine and their competitor's seven, they were doing very well. The fact that they should be getting 15 was difficult to comprehend."[68]

~

Though Welch's success may seem like an anomaly, it is characteristic of GE, says management consultant Tom Peters: "[E]very major internally grown business success at GE, from high-tech turbines to the GE Credit Corporation (GECC) and GE Information Services Company (GEISCO), came through a passionate champion, working within a skunk works operation, always at or slightly beyond the periphery of GE's formal policies and central systems."[69]

~

Welch next was named senior vice president and sector executive for the consumer products and services sector. At the same time, he became vice chairman of GE Credit Corporation. After 17 years in Pittsfield, Welch's family finally moved to Fairfield, Connecticut. The top job at GE lured him there:

> "[I]n '77, Reg called and said we're now going to go to this new configuration; he said, 'a race,' which was difficult for me. He said, 'If you don't come now, you won't be in the race, so you gotta come now.' So I moved down here, and went through that thing. I decided I wanted to become chairman. I would have liked to become chairman. Within two years of coming down, they named three vice-chairmen, and then two years later, they made me chairman." [70]

~

This is Reg Jones' version of the story: "I told him he had to get out of being a hick up in Massachusetts, running his own little bailiwick, with everybody genuflecting to him; that if he wanted to amount to

something, he had better get down here where the
real competition was going on."[71]

~

The competition turned into a fierce fight for domi-
nance. Of all the candidates, Welch was the least typical. GE-ers called him "someone who colored outside
the lines," even a "wild man." In one work evaluation,
Welch frankly stated his goal of becoming CEO, but
admitted he needed to work on his social skills. Still,
Jones liked what he saw: "We need entrepreneurs
who are willing to take well-considered business
risks—and at the same time know how to work in
harmony with a larger business entity. The intellectual requirements are light-years beyond the requirements of less complex organizations," Jones said.[72]

~

In December 1980, it was announced that Welch
would be the next chairman of GE, chosen over
nuclear engineer Edward E. Hood, 50, and physicist
John F. Burlingame, 58.

*"I think I'm the most happy man in America today,
and I'm certainly the most fortunate."[73]*

~

At 45, Welch was the youngest chief executive ever
appointed at GE. The company was 92 years old, but
Welch was only the eighth CEO.

~

Jones knew that Welch faced great challenges, so he left instructions: "Wall Streeters think of us as the aging wonder boys of the electromechanical age, but they're waiting to see whether we can make it into the electronics age. We're going to show them that General Electric is determined to be the beneficiary, not the victim, of the microelectronics revolution. You must all advance our technological renaissance."[74]

~

Though Welch expresses great respect for his predecessor, Reg Jones, he quickly made it clear that he was no Reg Jones. For example, he said that if management didn't move fast enough he would "kick ass," unlikely language from the courtly, British-born Jones.

Both Jones and Welch had style, but different styles. "Had Hollywood filmed the GE story, David Niven would have played Jones. Welch, by contrast, is the Spencer Tracy character," explained a *Barron*'s reporter.[75]

~

Welch says he arrived on the job with no master plan; and despite his brash ways, Welch found the job somewhat intimidating:

> *"When you're running an institution, you're always scared at first. You're afraid you might break it."*[76]

~

Not much for reminiscing, Welch nevertheless sometimes thinks of his early career at GE:

> "[T]here are days I sign things and push paper around on my desk and sit in meetings and go home knowing I didn't really do a helluva lot of anything . . . and I think back to the days when the plastics business was brand new . . . regarded as an upstart . . . flash in the pan . . . a bunch of maniacs. And every day you went home—if you did—knowing that big things had been done or at least tried. That is something wonderful, and it is an atmosphere we are trying to grow—or regrow—in every business in our company."[77]

~

Even if he does have occasional slow days, they don't last long and they don't dampen Welch's ardor:

> "I don't like this job. I love this job. If you like business and you like hanging around with bright, enthusiastic people—I love the team because I picked it all. Naturally, having been in it this long, they're my friends. . . . Yesterday I was in power systems all day; the day before I was in aircraft engines all day reviewing the [program]; and the day before that I was in plastics. Then I had NBC last week on Wednesday. We bought a company in the power field over the weekend. We bought an insurance company over the weekend. We settled a three-year contract with our labor unions over the weekend. It was very successful. Our sixth success without one disruption.

All weekend we were doing deals and another team was down there doing the union thing. It's a whole series of things, you know. It's such fun."[78]

TAKE THIS JOB AND DO IT

How many hours a day does it take to run GE?

"I spend enough hours to get the job done."[79]

∽

Welch starts his day with a three-mile walk, at a fast pace on a treadmill. A car picks him up just after 7:00 A.M. to take him to the office.

He sits on no outside corporate boards and focuses his day almost entirely on running GE. Welch often commutes in the corporate Sikorsky helicopter to GE's New York offices at Rockefeller Center or to the training center at Crotonville. He travels to Europe at least once a year, often in the spring, to visit GE facilities. Operating from a suite at Hotel Bristol in Paris, Welch reviews the activities of European managers. He goes to the Far East for several weeks each fall to tour plants and review operations in Asia.

∽

"I talk to the business leaders on the phone once a week to say, 'How are you doing?' See, we've been around. We all know each other. We like each other. We are the $60 billion, corner-grocery-store company. This may sound silly, but it's a neat place where a lot of people like hanging around."[80]

At meetings, Welch munches on fresh fruit and veg-etables, waving a strawberry or carrot stick in the air to make a point. He sketches madly on a napkin and rifles through reams of reports looking for the chart that illustrates his point. Welch is always on the move, and though he is a champion of the informa-tion age, he doesn't use a personal computer for his work: "I don't need one. I don't know what I'd do with it."[81]

When accused of cutting jobs and overworking those remaining, Welch replied:

> *"If someone tells me, 'I'm working 90 hours a week,' I say, 'You're doing something terribly wrong. I go skiing on the weekend; I got out with my buddies on Friday and party. You've got to do the same or you've got a bad deal. Put down a list of the 20 things you're doing that make you work 90 hours, and 10 of them have to be nonsense—or else some-body else has got to do them for you."[82]*

Finding the right managers and motivating them is Welch's single greatest task. Since Welch took over in 1981, he has personally okayed every general manager's slate of executives, some 500 positions in all. Richard Stonesifer, retired president and CEO of GE Appliances says that Welch "approves the salary increases of all the officers—of which there are 130 to 140—and person-ally controls the restricted-stock programs."[83]

~

Those are just the details. His real job, Welch says, is different:

"My job is to find great ideas, exaggerate them, and spread them like hell around the business with the speed of light."[84]

~

"I firmly believe my job is to walk around with a can of water in one hand and a can of fertilizer in the other and to make things flourish."[85]

QUALITIES OF A LEADER: WELCH STYLE

THE CHALLENGE: TO BE FAIR

"The biggest challenge is to be fair. No one trains you to be a judge."[86]

~

Honesty is essential, Welch says:

"Tell people the truth, because they know the truth anyway."[87]

~

Welch says that he expects GE employees to win, but to win honestly:

"Excellence and competitiveness are totally compatible with honesty and integrity. The A student, the four-minute miler, the high-jump record holder— all strong winners—can achieve those results without resorting to cheating. People who cheat are simply weak."[88]

~

"A professor gave a hypothetical case to his business school students. He said, 'If you were running a business for a larger company and were about to book a $50 million order, but to do so, you had to deposit $1 million in a Swiss bank account to an agent, would you do it?' Approximately 40 percent to 50 percent said they would. I was shocked! Shocked! I told the students someone was teaching them the wrong things. This was not one of those cases where you had to interpret the law; this was a simple bribery case."[89]

~

"In the end, your integrity is all you've got."[90]

~

NOTE: GE has had its share of scandals, though none have been linked to Welch. (For more, see "Dirty Diamonds and Other GE Scandals," in the next chapter.)

THE TEMPERAMENT OF A BOSS

"I am an optimist, someone who is often accused of seeing the glass as always half full. And I'm probably guilty as charged."[91]

~

"I don't think of myself as a risk taker. I think of myself as somebody who tries to do the careful analysis needed to make the right decisions—but

clearly one who is willing and anxious to make such decisions."[92]

~

Welch learned to be tenacious while doing graduate research at the University of Illinois.

"You go down 27,000 blind alleys. It doesn't work. You start again. You feel there's no hope while you're asking those questions, pressing, probing, pushing. But you have to get it resolved; otherwise you'd spend your whole life looking for the ultimate answer."[93]

~

Welch can be impatient. Tom Peters recalls this incident: "A story is told of Welch. He had asked some purchasing people to work on some tasks. Weeks later, he met with them to review their progress. To his dismay, they had none to report, only weighty analyses and half-completed efforts at coordination with various departments. Welch was furious. He called the meeting to an abrupt halt, then ordered it reconvened only four hours later. The agenda? To report on progress. He got it, too. More was done in those four hours than had been done in the several weeks preceding them."[94]

~

Organizational development expert Karl Weick points out a Welch paradox: "Welch makes real trouble for theorists of behavior commitment. To his top people, Welch says essentially, 'If I'm paying you $200K, I can damn well demand full commitment to change.' Research on behavioral commitment shows that people get committed to public, irrevocable, volitional acts. Maybe Welch is able to get commitment from people because he keeps reminding them, 'Look, you don't have to stay here and take this. You can go somewhere else.' If they stay, then they have acted out of their own volition."[95]

~

It may be clear to others, but Welch doesn't understand why he's called a tough boss:

> *"The people with whom I have been associated have worked harder, enjoyed it more—although not always initially—and in the end, gained increased self-respect from accomplishing more than they previously thought possible."[96]*

~

> *"My reputation for harshness is overblown. From the beginning, it was stamped into my forehead. Though to a certain extent it was understandable. I made changes that upset people's lives. They'd like somebody to blame."[97]*

~

> *"I have to be perceived as demanding. There are six companies going after every order out there. . . .*

There is an atmosphere of rigor at GE, but not of fear."⁹⁸

THE THRILL OF VICTORY

To Jack Welch, competition is not simply an episode that must be endured to achieve success, it is an ongoing, everyday state of affairs. And for Welch, that's fine, because when competition is at its keenest, he's living life at its fullest:

In 1994, Welch told the Economic Club of Detroit that the prosperous times being enjoyed by the United States only meant the country had reached the eye of a competitive hurricane. The United States had been through one side of the storm and another fierce round of international competition was coming:

> *"The paradox is that these brutally competitive times will be the most exciting, rewarding, and fulfilling for those fortunate enough to be part of boundaryless companies."*⁹⁹

∼

Later in the same speech to an audience dominated by auto makers, Welch sounded like a hockey coach telling players where to put the puck:

> *"We must concede no markets—and no customers— because our competitors do not. You [know] with car models, and I know with turbines and jet engines and CT medical scanners that there is a value nub,*

an intersection, where low-cost and just-the-right-features intersect. That value nub, when hit, causes products to fly off the shelves and out of the showrooms. The consuming passion of each of our companies must be to become so fast and so lean and so close to that customer that the value nub is always in our sights."[100]

~

"We come to work every day on the razor's edge of a competitive battle."[101]

~

At stake is the well-being of an entire nation. In the early 1980s, national productivity was in an alarming decline:

"U.S. business today finds itself challenged by aggressive overseas competitors. National productivity has been declining, and in industry after industry, product leadership is moving to other nations. Companies that refuse to renew themselves, that fail to cast off the old and embrace new technologies, could well find themselves in serious decline in the 1990s. We are determined that this shall not happen to General Electric."[102]

~

One GE division learned this lesson the hard way:

"At GE Power Systems—after decades of load growth and prosperity—the attitude toward customers

became: 'We make turbines. This is what we charge for them. Would you care for one?' It took a humbling order drought of several years to overcome that arrogance and make that business a customer-friendly one."[103]

~

Despite his obsession with competition, Welch does not merely scare workers into action with stories of the enemy. Organizational development expert Karl Weick observed another Welch paradox: "Welch apparently views the Japanese simultaneously as competitors, partners, friends, and enemies: This is a good example of not being forced into either/or thinking...."[104]

~

Welch believes shareholder activism puts U.S. companies on their toes:

"[W]hile some in this country often complain about share-owner activism, impatience, and demands for performance, I believe that the indulgence and the patience of the European and Japanese share owners has had the effect of lessening the bite, the urgency, and the overall competitive edge of their companies."[105]

~

Welch believes in "constructive conflict." If an idea can't stand up to an aggressive attack, it is a weak idea.

~

NBC executive Brandon Tartikoff said competition is what makes Jack Welch get up in the morning: "He's like me. He loves to win."[106]

NOTE: Tartikoff became the youngest entertainment president in network history when at age 30, he took over NBC's ailing programming and made it the most successful in the business. Tartikoff died in 1997 at the age of 48 of Hodgkin's disease.

A TYPICAL MEETING WITH CHAIRMAN WELCH

By most accounts, a meeting with Jack Welch is something like a Roadrunner cartoon. Jack dashes away chortling, "Wasn't that great?" His staff leaves the same meeting feeling like Wile E. Coyote—run over, blown up, dumped off a cliff. But it isn't so bad once you learn the game.

One employee explained: "You can't even say hello to Jack without it being confrontational. If you don't want to step up to Jack toe to toe, belly to belly, and argue your point, he doesn't have any use for you."[107]

～

John Opie, vice chairman of GE, says staffers prepare for meetings with Welch the way they would get ready for the big game: "You go in pumped up. You go in ready for combat." If Welch doesn't like your acquisition proposal, he might say, 'you're crazy, that's too much money; not even close. Go get it for half.'

You'd better have a thick skin, or when you come out, you will be a hurting person."[108]

~

David Orselet, a retired GE executive warns: "The one thing you can never do with Jack is wing it. If he ever catches you winging it, you're in trouble. Real trouble. You have to go in with in-depth information. Stand up for what you believe, but acknowledge what you don't know when you don't know it."[109]

~

Frank P. Doyle, former senior vice president for corporate relations once said: "It's a brawl; it's argumentative, confrontational. There's a much higher decibel level here. I told Jack what passes for conversation here would be seen as a mugging by RCA people."[110]

~

According to one former, unnamed GE executive: "Jack will chase you around the room, throwing arguments and objections at you. Then you fight back until he lets you do what you want—and it's clear you'll do everything you can to make it work. It's a ritual. It's like signing up."[111]

~

But if Welch really doesn't like your idea, you'll know it. Leonard Vickers, GE's former marketing vice president, tells about reviewing an ad agency presentation with Welch: "I was using my indirect English to tell the agency it wasn't on target. Jack just picked up the storyboard, threw it on the floor and said, 'See? We don't like it! It doesn't work!'"[112]

~

Dr. Steve Kerr, director of GE's leadership education center at Crotonville, says that when he first came to GE, people told him that the trouble with Welch is that he had a "shit list" of people who failed to impress him. Another employee agreed, then added, "But you can get off of it."

Kerr says that Welch sometimes does change his mind about employees, and will even promote them if they've overcome their damaged image.[113]

"He comes to judgement quickly," Kerr says. "If you are as opinionated as Jack, it's useful to be able to change your mind."[114]

~

Some observers claim that over time, GE executives have become increasingly deferential toward Welch, unwilling to stand up to him. A notable exception is Gary Wendt, head of GE's profit dynamo, GE Capital Services. If it weren't for his age, 55, and a highly publicized and contentious divorce, Wendt might be considered a candidate to replace Welch when he retires.

"Wendt is the only top executive at a GE function who won't be kissing Jack's ass," an unnamed retired GE executive was quoted as saying.[115]

~

Author Richard Tanner Pascale: "For those who know Welch personally, his blunt confronting style and his steamroller drive to succeed are more than offset by his sincerity, courage, and dedication. But strong leaders cast long shadows. The majority of GE managers 'see' Welch second- or third-hand. From a distance he can seem overbearing and instrumental."[116]

HUMOR US

You probably had to be there to know for sure if Jack Welch was joking. Welch is good friends with Henry Kissinger, but when Nancy Kissinger called to see whether Welch could help get an appliance repaired he cracked: "What do you think I am, a repairman?" Welch took care of the problem, and in recent years has made quality improvement his number one priority.

~

When asked if he agreed that he and the late GM chairman Alfred Sloan were the two greatest corporate executives of the century Welch said: "I didn't know Alfred Sloan."[117]

~

Welch admits that he is revered by some and reviled by others. Welch says that depending on whom you ask, he is "somewhere between a prince and a pig."[118]

~

Welch tells the story of an arrogant, pompous bullfrog who'd heard stories of other frogs being kissed by princesses and turned into handsome princes. "He figured he would be an excellent candidate. He went to a fortune-teller and told her he was sure a beautiful woman somewhere was looking for him. The fortune-teller looked into her crystal ball and sure enough, said, 'I see a beautiful young woman watching you ... exploring your body for hours ... driven to know everything about you.' 'I knew it,' said the frog. 'Where will I meet this woman?' The fortune-teller looked again into her crystal ball. 'In her biology lab,' she replied."[119]

∼

A clue to the temperament of Jack Welch is the fact that he is an unabashed fan of brash radio talk-show host Don Imus.

"There's a lot of Don in every one of us. Most of us don't have the guts to be Don. Our suits constrain us."[120]

WELCH'S WORLD: GENERAL ELECTRIC

THE ENGINE CALLED GENERAL ELECTRIC

At 119 years old, General Electric is one of the most profitable and powerful businesses in America. GE employs between 240,000 and 260,000 people who operate in more than 100 countries. The United States has only a handful of companies with the history and authority of GE. It is in a class with such ancient and influential Japanese conglomerates as Mitsubishi and Sumitomo, the European corporations Unilever and Nestle's, and deeply rooted American giants DuPont and the Coca-Cola Company.

Since its inception, GE has endured 19 presidents, 23 recessions, the Great Depression, six wars, and countless changes to the tax code. During that same time, GE has been awarded more patents than any other company in the United States.

~

Here is how Jack Welch sees the company:

"GE is a bubbling cauldron of ideas and learning, with tens of thousands of people playing alternate roles of teacher and student."[121]

~

Welch used the imagery of a business engine to illustrate how GE's various businesses fit together as a corporate entity. The engine is driven by the separate businesses, working together like pistons. The gasoline that fuels their performance is capital, which is regulated by top management. Earnings are the engine's thrust. The engine throws off spare cash to fund dividends, pay for acquisitions, and finance expansions.

Welch realizes that there are many concepts that describe GE. It depends on who is looking: its shareholders, customers, suppliers, employees, and even members of the society in which it operates.

~

"GE is about the closest approximation of the American economy in microcosm—with roughly one-third of our earnings in services, in high tech, and in some smokestack manufacturing . . ."[122]

~

Economists once believed that since GE reflected the U.S. economy, it could grow at no faster a rate than the economy in general. Welch realized there were ways to beat the GNP limitations; for example, to be better than the average United States company and to expand globally.

Though Welch refused to accept the growth limitations of a GNP company, he did structure GE similarly to the United States, operating as a political democracy (or nearly so) with a capitalist economy. That, he said, gives a competitive advantage.

> *"What our system has is freedom. It allows people like me to become chairman of GE in one generation, it allows the talented young engineers in our company to move up fast. If we put bureaucracy and rigidness into our system, we play into our competitors' hands in global markets."*[123]

Welch has changed the way GE looks from the customer's perspective:

> *"At one time, GE executives spent more time on company politics than they did on actual business. People said that GE operated with its face to the CEO and its ass to the customer."*[124]

In the new world environment, Welch says, a company cannot provide job security. Only customers can do that:

> *"One thing we've discovered with certainty is that anything we do that makes that customer more successful inevitably results in a financial return for us."*[125]

~

Welch revolutionized the relationship between companies and their workers, says Daniel McGlaughlin, former head of GE's computer-aided design subsidiary. In past years, McGlaughlin says, GE employees were paid whether they worked or not. "But [Welch] brought in a new kind of contract, one where the company supplies the opportunity, resources, and environment, and the workers supply the skills and energy."[126]

~

It all came back to that familiar word: competition:

> *"The new psychological contract, if there is such a thing, is that jobs at GE are the best in the world for people who are willing to compete. We have the best training and development resources and an environment committed to providing opportunities for personal and professional growth."*[127]

~

To critics who say GE's work environment has lost its humanity, Welch insists the company is "hard-headed but warmhearted."[128]

~

> *"The job of the enterprise is to provide an exciting atmosphere that's open and fair, where people have the resources to go out and win. The job of the people is to take advantage of this playing field and put out 110 percent."*[129]

~

While facing economic realities, GE managers still must care about the people who work for them:

"If they don't go out and care about their people, the people won't do things for them. You have to constantly show that you care. The only thing that makes our company work is the fact that our people are in the game. We don't do it."[130]

~

Although Welch dwells less on serving stockholders than other CEOs do, equity holders are never far from his mind:

"A proper balance between shareholders, employees, and communities is what we all try to achieve. But it is a tough balancing act because, in the end, if you don't satisfy shareholders, you don't have the flexibility to do the things you have to do to take care of employees or communities. In our society, like it or not, we have to satisfy shareholders."[131]

~

Shareholders have been well rewarded. GE stock purchased for $100 when Jack Welch became chairman in 1981 would be worth $2,194.30 today. Return to shareholders has averaged 23 percent a year. During that time, GE's share price increase was nearly double that of the Dow Jones industrial average and 76 percent higher than the Standard & Poor's 500 stock index.

~

Welch has a boss, too: GE's board of directors:

> *"I think the board's job is to hire a chairman and CEO in charge of the whole company and to hold him to a high standard; and if that person isn't delivering, to remove him. It's probably the board's biggest responsibility. Know where the company's going. Pick the person. Then get out of the way. And if he doesn't deliver, call him in and say, 'go home, go to the beach.'"* [132]

~ ✴ ~

GE: JUST AN EVERYDAY $79 BILLION FAMILY STORE?

GENERAL ELECTRIC'S FINANCIAL POSITION, MAY 15, 1997

TOTAL ASSETS:	$272.4 billion
TOTAL REVENUES:	$79.18 billion (up 13 percent from previous year)
EARNINGS:	$7.3 billion (up 11 percent from previous year)
MARKET VALUE OF GE STOCK:	$200 billion, the highest market value in the world. Shares traded at around $65.
EMPLOYEES WORLDWIDE:	Approximately 260,000

GE IN 1981: THE BEGINNING OF
THE WELCH REVOLUTION

TOTAL ASSETS: $20 billion

REVENUES: $27.24 billion

EARNINGS: $1.65 billion

MARKET VALUE OF GE STOCK: $12 billion, 11th in the
United States. Shares,
adjusted for splits, were
trading at around $4.

EMPLOYEES WORLDWIDE: 440,000

BEYOND NATIONAL BORDERS

By the year 2000, half of all GE's revenues will be generated abroad.

In 1989, Welch boasted that:

> *"A full 40 percent of GE's operating profits today flow from outside the United States ... [A]nd the demand for our products and services allowed us to make a $3.1 billion positive contribution to the U.S. balance of trade in 1988."*[133]

Welch saw vast opportunities at the end of the Cold War:

> *"Half a century of wars, fear, hate, and huge defense spending burdens is over. And the opportunities of an increasingly peaceful world await us. Russia, Eastern Europe, and China have gone from military targets to market opportunities overnight. Peace is breaking out all over the world. Borders and markets are* opening up, *creating vast opportunities for fast, creative, competitive companies."[134]*

～

> *"If you're not in Germany, you're not in Europe. And if you're not in Asia, you're nowhere."[135]*

～

Some people call GE a mature business, with limited future growth, but Welch says globalization makes that concept outdated:

> *"What business could be mature when you have economies with more than 2 billion people in India, China, and Southeast Asia?"[136]*

～

> *"Mexico is booming, with a government dedicated to open markets, with imports that will grow from $40 billion last year [1992] to $115 billion by 2000. From New York or Raleigh, Mexico is a shorter flight than Los Angeles, and it is a market America*

*can't miss. Southeast Asia has a GNP that is dou-
bling every decade with enormous infrastructure
and technology needs made for American businesses
that can compete. India, with close to 125 million
middle-class consumers and an exciting new government commitment to market liberalization, represents a vast opportunity for the next century. Sure
they are far away. Sure the cultures are different.
And that's why only those passionately devoted to
growth are going to share in the huge rewards of
winning in these markets."*[137]

~

*"We [the United States] and Mexico have to be part-
ners; we have to find a way together to make Mexico
work. My belief is that Mexico is a great country
and will be a great country."*[138]

~

When asked how GE deals with cultural differences
when operating in so many parts of the world, Welch
shrugged:

*"Cultural differences I don't worry about. I think the
question to any one of those things is, 'What are the
alternatives?' I mean, the facts are that if you're not
in that part of the world, participating, feeling, getting ideas, touching, smelling it, they're [the competi-
tors] going to come get you. You've got to be in every
market. People say, 'You're taking too big a risk in*

China.' What are my alternatives? Stay out? China may not make it, and we may not make it in China. But there's no alternative to being in there with both feet, participating in this huge market, with this highly intelligent crowd of people. We don't know China. Every time I leave China, I know how much I don't know. I was there three times last year. We ran a best practices study. We talked to a zillion firms. We know this much: We're going to be there."[139]

～

"We're all in the global arena now and there isn't even the usual one-minute break between rounds in this battle."[140]

HEROS

In companies like GE, Welch says:

"The hero is the one with the ideas."[141]

～

GE had plenty of historic characters of its own—inventor Thomas Edison, legendary engineer Charles Steinmetz, and Charles Coffin, who became head of GE when investors forced Edison out. Coffin is known as the father of professional management. These heros helped bond the organization together under a common history and culture and were role models to those who followed.

～

Fred Borch became GE's CEO at about the time Welch joined the company and according to Welch, was right for his time:

> *"Borch let a thousand flowers bloom. He got us into modular housing and entertainment businesses, nurtured GE Credit through its infancy, embarked on ventures in Europe, and left Aircraft Engine and Plastics alone so they could really get started. It became evident after he stepped down that GE had once again established a foothold into some businesses with a future."[142]*

~

Welch has found inspiration outside GE. He sometimes quotes Helmuth von Moltke, a nineteenth century Prussian general who served as military advisor to the Ottoman court. Von Moltke wrote that detailed military strategies invariably were foiled by unexpected events once a battle began:

> *"Von Moltke believed strategy was not a lengthy action plan, but rather the evolution of a central idea through continually changing circumstances."[143]*

~

> *"Sam Walton was an authentic American hero, certainly one of mine. But for one group of folks, he has been nothing but trouble—those managers of mature businesses, of whatever size, whose standby excuse for stagnation is that their markets are mature, and there-*

fore it's all beyond their control. What Sam Walton did was to go into one of the most mature industries of all and find a way to make it grow, grow, grow, double-digit, month after month, year after year. He did it by innovation, customer focus, and above all, speed."[144]

~

Welch has been influenced by Peter Drucker, who has served as a consultant to GE and a lecturer at Crotonville:

"[W]e have got to ask ourselves Peter Drucker's very tough question, 'If you weren't already in the business, would you enter it today?' And if the answer is no, face into that second difficult question, 'What are you going to do about it?'"[145]

THE HOLY CITY

No sooner was Welch named chairman of GE, than he buttonholed Jim Baughman, then head of GE's Management Development Institute at Crotonville, New York, and said:

"I want a revolution, and I want it to start at Crotonville."[146]

Crotonville, with its woodsy, 52-acre campus high above the Hudson River, has played a central role in GE culture, but Welch wanted it to become even more influential.

~

As early as the 1950s, GE's leadership realized that its management training needs were unique. Chairman Ralph Cordiner purchased the estate of the Hopf Institute in Ossining, New York, where he built the first private corporate training center. Crotonville now has many imitators, including IBM's Sands Point School and Hitachi's Management Development Institute in Japan. Called "the Harvard of corporate America" Crotonville's official mission is ". . . to seek solutions for GE today and develop leaders for GE tomorrow."

~

"We strive for the antithesis of blind obedience. We want people to have the self-confidence to express opposing views, get all the facts on the table, and respect differing opinions. It is our preferred mode of learning; it's how we form balanced judgments. We value the participation, involvement, and conviction this approach breeds."[147]

~

Education, whether at Crotonville or elsewhere, is a priority for Welch. GE spends $500 million a year on education and training, and that figure will double by the end of this century.

~

Considering that every new GE manager goes there for at least two and a half days, and that 5,000 employees, customers, and suppliers attend each year, Crotonville is small. Deer meander on the former farm just north of Tarrytown. On a clear day, New York City's World Trade Center shimmers on the horizon, some 30 miles away. A knoll at the entrance to the campus is dominated by a helicopter pad—a subtle reminder that Chairman Jack Welch might arrive momentarily.

Crotonville has the trappings of an understated but pricey resort. At every door are stands full of golf umbrellas. If it's raining people just take one, dash to the next building, and leave it there. Bouquets of fresh flowers; bowls of grapes, plums, apples, and bananas; and coffee bars are scattered throughout the buildings. Every restroom has a bottle of mouthwash and stacks of tiny disposable cups.

Four buildings accommodate 146 resident students. In addition to the main dining room, the residence hall has a fully supplied pantry so that guests, who sometimes are suffering jet lag from Asia or Europe, can grab a soda or an ice cream bar, or heat up soup or a frozen pizza anytime of the day or night. There is an open liquor bar at the recreation building. There are no cash registers anywhere on campus.

Dr. Steve Kerr, current dean of Crotonville, admits there is something called "Crotonville creep," the average two-pound weight gain for every week spent there. "As they say at GE," jokes Kerr, "If it's worth doing, it's worth over doing."[148]

~

Every GE-er who comes to Crotonville knows about "the pit," a small, intimate auditorium where the speaker stands in a well-like depth, with a semicircular theater rising around the podium. Named after Welch's favorite childhood play spot, the pit is GE's Greek forum. Welch bans reporters, security analysts, and most other outsiders from the pit to encourage the free flow of ideas—and because, when there, Welch says almost anything that comes to his mind.

～

Welch teaches a leadership class at Crotonville, usually once a month. "It would have been a waste of his time, but he'd be a great professor," observes Kerr.[149]

～

GE also takes its Crotonville-style programs to Japan and other distant locations and offers "virtual" Crotonville training in various electronic modes. Kerr also is planning permanent Crotonville clones in Europe.

～

Kerr, a former professor at the University of Michigan and dean of the faculty at the University of Southern California Business School, explains that many of the concepts used at Crotonville are borrowed. "Crotonville has not contributed much to the theory of management, but it has contributed enormously to the practice," Kerr says.

Even GE's famous workout program borrows heavily from the concepts of participative management and Japanese quality circles. "Crotonville has this Camelot reputation of being a mecca for leadership development, but in fact we do some things extremely well, others less well. There isn't any secret sauce here. Our strength is not that we do cutting edge stuff, but we implement that very well."[150]

When asked if Crotonville is as good as its reputation, Kerr says perhaps not. "Nothing could be," Kerr says, "It has a Camelot reputation." Nevertheless, Kerr says he and his Crotonville faculty are "diligent students" of the art of management.[151]

Indeed, Crotonville has served in the role that Welch hoped it would when he became CEO: "It was the glue that held things together as the process of change took hold."[152]

GE JARGON

Every culture has its language, and Jack Welch's GE is no different. Many business catchwords, phrases, and acronyms either originated at or were popularized by GE. They have leaked out and spread everywhere. The following is a partial list:

Bullet train: GE's approach to change. You can increase the speed of the bullet train somewhat by making modifications, but if you want it to go a lot faster, you have to make radical changes to the design of the train and the system on which it runs.

MBO: Management by objectives was developed jointly by Peter Drucker and GE. Under MBO, each manager was responsible for a profit center and was expected to achieve his or her hurdle rates; in GE's case, 7 percent return on sales and 20 percent return on investment. Its fatal flaw: the tendency of managers to "harvest" a business, depleting it long-term for short-term gains. By the time the business had imploded, the manager already had been promoted and was no longer associated with the problems. When several senior GE executives were accused of price-fixing in 1959, it was suspected that they were motivated by pressure to meet difficult objectives.

SBU: The organization of a business by strategic business units.

Smart bombing: The process of overseas marketing in which GE studies each country separately, in detail, then arranges a mix of products, brands, manufacturing facilities, marketing, and retail strategies to maximize performance in each. This method is in keeping with a familiar GE mantra "We manage markets, not factories."[153]

Strategic planning: An old GE term for a sophisticated approach to anticipating the future and positioning a company to make the best of changing circumstances. GE now talks about CAP or change acceleration process.

SWOT analysis: A way entrepreneurs can analyze any new opportunity or challenge. When you understand the strength, weaknesses, opportunities, and threats inherent in a situation, you are better prepared to make a decision. Over the years, GE managers also learned to solve problems by fishbone and force-field analyses, two popular management tools.

TPC: The analysis of business issues in technical, political, and cultural terms.

POIM: A strategy developed by GE management in the 1950s, but now out of vogue. It stands for plan, organize, integrate, and measure.

～

Welch, though it may not have been his intention to expand the language, has brought some of the most feared words to the American workplace.

Downsizing: Or more nicely put, right-sizing. Either way, it means to disemploy people.

Rationalization: To reorganize a business so that it is more efficient, which usually means fewer employees.

Welch would like the business world to adopt his definition of "company loyalty":
"Loyalty is an affinity among people who want to

grapple with the outside world and win. Their personal values, dreams, and ambitions cause them to gravitate toward each other and toward a company like GE that gives them the resources and opportunities to flourish."[154]

DIRTY DIAMONDS AND OTHER GE SCANDALS

Under Jack Welch's watch as CEO, General Electric has experienced its share of scandal. In 1985, federal prosecutors in Philadelphia charged GE's Re-Entry Systems with 108 counts of criminal fraud, claiming that managers responsible for building a new nose cone for the Air Force's Minuteman nuclear missile system had altered workers' time cards, cheating the government of $800,000. Incorrect numbers were entered on approximately 100 of the 100,000 time cards submitted for the project over a three-year period.

GE was immediately, though temporarily, suspended from doing business with the U.S. government—even from selling lightbulbs to Uncle Sam. The company risked losing more than $5 billion in revenues.

At first, GE claimed there was no wrongdoing. Then, on further investigation, a different story emerged. GE eventually pleaded guilty to the charges.

"The most gut-wrenching thing was being battered in the defense scandal. It hurt, it hurt a lot. We love this place and somebody was throwing stones at it. We went down a lot of paths [figuring out what happened]. It takes a long time because [people] come in with arguments about the complexity of government rules and a lot of other things. Then we got to the point where we concluded that someone did cheat, someone did try to beat the system. Until we got to that point, we were chasing ourselves around in a circle. But it isn't the government's fault. It's basic integrity."[155]

~

GE scandal often involves military contracts, which frequently resemble the plots for international-intrigue novels. In early 1980s, Israeli Air Force General Rami Dotan was convicted in his own country for colluding with GE Aircraft Engines employees to divert more than $30 million of U.S. government funds for battlefield computer systems to their personal accounts. The GE employees were fined $10 million and sent to jail. GE cooperated with the investigation and signed a $69 million settlement with the U.S. government.

~

Spy novelist John LeCarre could have written the tale that unfolded when GE was accused of colluding to fix prices on industrial diamonds. The story began in

September 1991 when, with his characteristic bluntness, Jack Welch wrote a memo to Glen Hiner, then head of GE Plastics. "Russell has to go. He made a fool of himself in July, and yesterday he appeared totally out of it."[156]

Edward Russell, head of GE's diamond unit in Worthington, Ohio, did not take his dismissal quietly. Instead, he paid a call on the FBI office in Columbus, where he said GE and a Swiss subsidiary of the DeBeers Group were fixing prices on industrial diamonds. (The two companies account for nearly 80 percent of world sales of the diamonds, which are used in cutting tools.) Accusations about partying, prostitutes, and high-living GE executives were widely circulated.

Russell claimed that he got the axe for trying to bring the price-fixing scheme to the attention of top GE executives. In April 1992, Russell filed a wrongful dismissal lawsuit against GE and unleashed an international U.S. Justice Department investigation. Justice agents prowled the world, searching offices in Belgium in an attempt to indict German and Belgian businesspeople. They intercepted James Whitehead in customs as he returned to the United States for a golf tournament. He was whisked to Columbus to testify before a federal grand jury. Later, he voluntarily returned to the United States for the trial, where he modified his testimony somewhat.

When asked why he changed his story, Whitehead explained: "Well, you arrested me, you imprisoned me, and you put me on a late night plane. I didn't arrive here until early in the morning, and I got no sleep that night. So, my recollection possibly wasn't at its best."[157]

Russell's suit against GE never went to trial. Two of Russell's wrongful dismissal charges against GE were dismissed by a judge. Welch and a lawyer met with Russell for lunch and negotiated an out-of-court settlement on a third and final accusation. In withdrawing his suit, Russell signed an affidavit saying his firing was not related to price-fixing and that he had no personal knowledge of antitrust wrongdoing.

Nonetheless, the Justice Department continued to pursue the case, but in December 1994, a federal judge in Columbus dismissed the charges. After hearing five weeks of government testimony, the judge said the case was too weak to place before a jury. Slim on proof, he said, "the government's conspiracy theory falls apart completely."[158]

∼

Welch says that it is unlikely that GE has been able to hire the only people who don't steal, cheat, take drugs, or engage in other unacceptable behavior:

"Whether it was a price-fixing scandal in the 1960s, a bribery case in the 1970s, or a defense timecard issue in the 1980s, a company of 300,000 to 400,000 people always has to be vigilant. [A]ll the practices and all the paper in the world will never stop one or

*two individiuals from going outside the corral. Our
job—everybody's job—is to talk integrity, preach
integrity, and, in every instance, live integrity."*[159]

~

The problem with the Re-Entry System time cards
prompted Welch to initiate an ethics program, which
is spelled out in a GE booklet, *The Spirit and the Letter
of Our Commitment.*

> *"It's in every language. We tell [employees] exactly
> who to call. We've got ombudspeople in every plant,
> and they have a hotline. That came out of the
> $800,000 time-card incident. We wouldn't have done
> that. Out of messes you create new levels of excel-
> lence. Something has to come out of every serious
> event. What did you learn? How do you [deal with]
> it? How do you take it to the next step?"*[160]

~

Business practices differ in other countries, making
U.S. legal standards difficult to follow, yet Welch says
it can be done:

> *"In a global business, you can win without bribes.
> But you better have technology. That's why we win
> in businesses like turbines, because we have the best
> gas turbine. You've got to be the low-priced supplier;
> but in almost all cases, if you have quality, price,
> and technology, you win—and nobody can sleaze-
> ball you."*[161]

~

Every worker is given "the spirit and the letter." It
starts with a message from Welch, which in part,
reads:

> *"Integrity is the rock upon which we build our busi-
> ness success—our quality products and services, our
> forthright relations with customers and suppliers,
> and ultimately, our winning competitive record.
> GE's quest for competitive excellence begins and
> ends with our commitment to ethical conduct."*[162]

THE FABRIC
OF LEADERSHIP

BE A LEADER, NOT A MANAGER

Welch's predecessor at GE, Reginald Jones compared the company's momentum to that of a supertanker: "Once you get it on course, you have to get out of the way or you get run down."[163]

Welch says passion provides the momentum:

"The world of the 1990s and beyond will not belong to 'managers' or those who can make the numbers dance. The world will belong to passionate, driven leaders—people who not only have enormous amounts of energy but who can energize those whom they lead."[164]

~

"In an environment where we must have every good idea from every man and woman in the organization, we cannot afford management styles that suppress and intimidate."[165]

~

71

"Weak managers destroy jobs. They are the killers of business; they are job killers."[166]

~

When it was suggested that he was down on managers, Welch replied:

"I simply dislike the traits that have come to be associated with 'managing'—controlling, stifling people, keeping them in the dark, wasting their time on trivia and reports. Breathing down their necks. You can't manage self-confidence into people. You have to get out of their way and let it grow in them by allowing them to win, and then rewarding them when they do. The word manager has too often come to be synonymous with control—cold, uncaring, button-down, passionless. I never associate passion with the word manager, and I've never seen a leader without it."[167]

~

Welch's ideal leader?

"Somebody who can develop a vision of what he or she wants their business unit, their activity to do and be. Somebody who is able to articulate to the entire unit what the business is, and gain through a sharing of discussion—listening and talking—an acceptance of the vision. And [someone who] then can relentlessly drive implementation of that vision to a successful conclusion."[168]

~

"Above all else, good leaders are open. They go up, down, and around their organizations to reach people. They don't stick to established channels. They're informal. They're straight with people. They make a religion out of being accessible."[169]

~

"[I]n small companies, with fewer layers and less camouflage, the leaders show up very clearly on the screen. Their performance and its impact are clear to everyone."[170]

~

Based on his own experience, Welch offers leaders some advice:

"One of the things about leadership is that you cannot be a moderate, balanced, thoughtful, careful articulator of policy. You've got to be on the lunatic fringe."[171]

~

"It's best to present big ideas without time frames or rigidly defined goals, because there is resistance to every idea that's different from the current norm. If you allow the naysayers to measure and quantify your idea, they can come back and blow it away before it has a chance to work."[172]

~

73

Welch is credited with moving from "command and control" style of leadership to a more interactive mode.

"I don't run GE. I lead GE."[173]

NO IDEAS DU JOUR

"Leaders—and you take anyone from Roosevelt to Churchill to Reagan—inspire people with clear visions of how things can be done better."[174]

$\sim$

When you have a vision, stick with it:

"If you have an idea du jour, you're dead."[175]

$\sim$

At a 1981 meeting with securities analysts at the Pierre Hotel in New York, Welch warned reporters not to confuse vision with strategy:

"If I could, this would be the appropriate moment for me to withdraw from my pocket a sealed envelope containing the grand strategy for the General Electric Company over the next decade. But I can't, and I am not going to attempt, for the sake of intellectual neatness, to tie a bow around the many diverse initiatives of General Electric . . . It just doesn't make sense for neatness sake to shoehorn these plans into an all-inclusive central strategy.

"What will enhance the many decentralized plans and initiatives of this company isn't a central

strategy, but a central idea—a simple core concept that will guide General Electric in the '80s and govern our diverse plans and strategies."[176]

~

Reporters didn't get it, perhaps because the vision was big and fuzzy around the edges. It was difficult to draw a straight line from what he said to corporate growth and profits:

"We are trying to get the soul and energy of a start-up into the body of a $60-billion, 114-year-old company."[177]

~

"The job for big companies, the challenge that we all face as bureaucrats, is to create an environment where people can reach their dreams—and they don't have to do it in a garage."[178]

~

"We set out to shape a global enterprise that preserved the classic big-company advantages, while eliminating the classic big-company drawbacks. What we wanted to build was a hybrid, an enterprise with the reach and resources of a big company—the body of a big company—but with the thirst to learn, the compulsion to share, and the bias for action—the soul—of a small company."[179]

~

"Our challenge is to make General Electric have all the benefits of a big company; and yet act with the speed, decisiveness, and knowledge of a small company."[180]

~

"[W]e all know what we want out of a small company. We know the characteristics: informality, lack of layers, getting close to the customers, making everybody's actions feel like they're important so they [consider] the implications of their actions."[181]

~

Though Welch wants GE to have small-company vitality, he does not want it to be small. He wrote in the GE 1995 annual report:

"Breaking up is the right answer for some big companies. For us, it is the wrong answer."[182]

~

Being large gives GE remarkable staying power:

"We make good use of the reach and the resources— financial, technological, and educational—of a big company. If fact, we intend to get bigger. But we have been fighting to eliminate or prevent the terrible by-products of bigness: the arrogance, the bureaucracy, the pomposity, and the stifling layers that are the common but controllable maladies of large institutions."[183]

~

"[B]eing big and agile is better than being small and agile. The only reason people are small is they can't get big. Nobody wants to stay small. The objective is to grow."[184]

~

Welch gave GE a small-company atmosphere by steps. First he modified GE's structure, then he changed the way GE employees think about their jobs:

"We want a company that focuses on nothing but serving customers, a company where everyone feels the thrill of winning and shares in its rewards—in the soul as well as the pocketbook."[185]

~

"We've got to take out the boss element. We're going to win on our ideas, not by whips and chains."[186]

~

It took several years before GE employees understood Welch's vision. Glen Hiner, a GE executive who worked with Welch in the plastics division said: "I think Jack had the vision very early, and he articulated the vision almost immediately. The trouble was, he expected to get everything done quickly. He didn't understand how big GE was. He didn't understand how deep he had to go to effect these changes. Even today, I think he continues to be amazed by the questions he gets asked at Crotonville, the ongoing lack of understanding."[187]

Welch finally accepted that it would take time to get his vision across:

> *"I hope you understand that business is a series of trial-and-error. It's not a great science. Mistakes are made. It's just moving the ball forward, and nobody has any great formula. If we have any one formula, it's that we believe that you've got to involve everyone in the game. You can't let any one mind guard the game. And we work on that every day, and everybody has to play, and more people [have to] share in the victory of the game. We have more pizza parties, we have more beer parties, we break open more kegs than anybody you can find. Because we try to get everybody to feel it isn't drudgery, it isn't going to the mundane, this is fun. You spend most of your waking hours at work. How do you create an atmosphere where it's exciting and fun and rewarding, intellectually, in the soul as well as the wallet?"*[188]

> *"The leader's unending responsibility must be to remove every detour, every barrier to ensure that vision is first clear, and then real."*[189]

E. Kirby Warren, management professor at Columbia University, says Welch's vision is pretty simple: "He says: 'Enough of this *In Search of Excellence* stuff. Let's *be* excellent.'"[190]

THE TRAP: MEASURING EVERYTHING, UNDERSTANDING NOTHING

"Too often we measure everything and understand nothing. The three most important things you need to measure in a business are customer satisfaction, employee satisfaction, and cash flow. If you're growing customer satisfaction, your global market share is sure to grow, too. Employee satisfaction feeds you productivity, quality, pride, and creativity. And cash flow is the pulse—the key vital sign of a company."[191]

Welch says that projections and budgets are dangerous, because they are made cautiously and conservatively and end up placing limits on success:

"I can't stand predictions. What I have to do is try to visualize the world, and I have to be agile enough to live with it and win in it. It doesn't mean a thing to say I'm going to do it. It only means something to do it."[192]

"Rigorous budgeting alone is nonsense. I think in terms of goals, in terms of the best you can do."[193]

"Figures are just the results. We've never made dollars our goal. Profits will flow from the success of this project."[194]

DON'T SELL HATS TO EACH OTHER

Until a company faces the truth, it can't move forward:

"Our issue is facing reality about having a troubled business situation. We [top managers] can take good news and we can take bad news. We're big people and we've been paid well, all of us. Don't sell hats to each other."[195]

In other words, be honest about what you're doing:

"An awful lot of ritual goes on in companies. A lot of what I call 'selling hats to each other,' They come in with big thick books, make presentations to each other; no customers know you're making it, the market doesn't know you've tied yourself up in a room preparing charts for weeks; so I constantly say, 'don't sell hats to each other,' go out and do business."[196]

$\sim$

"Don't finesse the numbers; tell it like it is, address the harsh realities of your situations."[197]

$\sim$

Welch *helps* GE workers face reality by telling them the truth—especially the painful truth In his 1993 annual meeting Welch told the audience:

"Our appliance business is profitable, but its head-quarters location at Louisville has a significant cost disadvantage versus its competitors. We're losing money at that plant—and everyone knows it—and we can't stay there if we can't get our total costs down."

He continued:

"Whether we win or lose in Louisville remains to be seen, but what is certain is that there will not be a man or woman in our Louisville operation who will not have access to all the facts—or will not have a chance to contribute to winning."

Welch then delivered the same chilling message to GE's electric motor business workers in Fort Wayne, Indiana, where the annual meeting was held:

"While this business overall is modestly profitable, the operations here in high-cost Fort Wayne are los-ing money. Our primary competition is Emerson, whose costs, because of plant relocations, are signifi-cantly less than our own. This company cannot run operations that are chronic money losers—whether they be in Louisville or Fort Wayne or anywhere."[198]

Welch ended his comments with encouraging words on the power of workers to overcome, but surely Welch's speech alarmed most of the residents of Fort Wayne.

~

NOTE: There are approximately 1,600 employees at the GE plant in Fort Wayne, and the facility is currently making money. For Louisville, see "It All Comes Out in the Wash."

~

In a 1986 session at Crotonville, a manager from the floundering factory automation business asked what would happen to his unit. Welch replied:

> *"If I were you, I'd get my resume ready. I know you don't want to hear that. But we're not making it in that business. To be fair to you, you've got to face that."*[199]

Later in the evening at a cocktail party, Welch made a point of talking with the manager, to make sure he was able to handle the bad news.

~

> *"Clearly, having everyone in a particular business understand the way the world really is, not the way they wished it were, having everyone prepared to deal with the future, is critical to competitive success."*[200]

~

Welch is adamant that GE-ers look forward, not back. At the 1990 shareholder's meeting, he briefly listed the accomplishments of the past decade, then told the audience:

"But as successful as the '80s were for GE, they're over, *and our energies must be focused on the '90s."*[201]

~

"[D]welling on the achievements and events of the past is not something we spend much time on at GE."[202]

SHARE INFORMATION

"Walter Wriston told me the day I got this job, 'Jack, remember one thing: you're always going to be the last one to know the critical things that need to be done in your organization. Everyone else already knows.' He was right."[203]

~

Welch has tried to eliminate communication filters that keep information from top management. His corporate executive council (CEC) meets for two days each quarter to help the heads of GE's major businesses know what's going on throughout the company:

"For me, good communication is simply everyone having the same set of facts. When everyone has the same facts, they can get involved in shaping the plans for their components. At the CEC, everyone in the room sees the entire company and can draw his or her own conclusions about its performance, its environment, where it's going for the next 90 days,

where it's going for the next two years, and where the vulnerabilities are, where the strengths are."[204]

~

Equally important, Welch wants information to flow freely from bottom to top and back again:

"The bureaucratic paraphernalia that often slows and impedes communications and discourages the innovator and the risk-taker has been swept aside; in its place a faster-moving, more action-oriented, and personally more satisfying environment has taken shape."[205]

~

"We are out to get a feeling and a spirit of total openness. That's alien to a manager of 25 or 30 years ago who got ahead by knowing a little more than the employee who works for him [or her]."[206]

~

"Openness is critical. We soon discovered how essential it is for a multibusiness company to become an open, learning organization. The ultimate competitive advantage lies in an organization's ability to learn and rapidly transform that learning into action. It may acquire that learning in a variety of ways—through great scientists, great management practices, or great marketing skills—but then it must rapidly assimilate its new learning and drive it."[207]

~

Even upstarts should have a voice:

*"We must have some of the freshness, the irrever-
ence, the desire to challenge and question that comes
from those who are impatient, who buck the system,
who can see the possibilities of a fresh start."*[208]

~

In a 1987 speech to employees, Welch said:

*"We've learned a bit about what communication is
not. It's not a speech like this or a videotape. It's not a
plant newspaper. Real communication is an attitude,
an environment. It's the most interactive of all
processes. It requires countless hours of eyeball-to-
eyeball back and forth. It involves more listening
than talking. It is a constant, interactive process
aimed at (creating) consensus."*[209]

~

As wonderful as this openness sounds, communicating
with Welch can be like getting a splash in the face
with ice water. Paul Van Orden, head of the consumer
section at GE, was struggling with declining quality,
high prices, and lower profitability at the major appliances division. Van Orden met Welch in the hallway
one day:

"How are you doing," Welch asked. "How
are things at majors?"

"They're really struggling, Jack," replied
Van Orden.

"Hey, is there anything I can do to help?" said Welch.

Van Orden thought for a minute then replied: "Yeah. You can stop referring to majors as a cesspool."

"I'll call it anything I like," Welch snapped back.

"Well," said Van Orden amiably, "thanks for all the help."[210]

THE CREED

It took some 5,000 GE employees three years to hammer out GE's value statement, with input from Welch. An early draft of the statement, circulated in 1989, encouraged employees to understand and embrace GE's values. But: "[I]ndividuals whose values do not coincide with these expressed preferences will more likely flourish better outside the General Electric Company."[211]

The so-called "flourish off" statement horrified many people at GE. Agree with us or get lost? Whatever happened to debate and dissent, they wondered?

When GE-ers confronted Welch with their views, they wore T-shirts with the GE "meatball" logo and the line, "Subscribe to our values or else." Welch got the message and dropped that part of the value statement.[212]

Reaching consensus, Welch said, "was a brutal process." But the value statement is so important to him that Welch carries it with him on a laminated card.[213] It reads:

GE leaders, always with unyielding integrity:

* Create a clear, simple, reality-based customer-focused vision, and are able to communicate it straightforwardly to all constituencies.

* Reach, set aggressive targets, recognize and reward progress, while understanding accountability and commitment.

* Have a passion for excellence, hate bureaucracy, and all the nonsense that comes with it.

* Have the self-confidence to empower others and behave in a boundaryless fashion; believe in and are committed to workout as a means of empowerment, are open to ideas from anywhere.

* Have, or have the capacity to develop, global brains and global sensitivity, and are comfortable building diverse and global teams.

* Have enormous energy and the ability to energize and invigorate others, stimulate and relish change, and not be frightened or paralyzed by it, see change as an opportunity, not a threat.

* Possess a mind-set that drives quality, cost, and speed for a competitive advantage.[214]

~

True, GE's value statement could have used a clear-minded, simplicity-based, grammar-focused copy editor. But this is a company of scientists and engineers, not English teachers.

~

Welch expects all GE employees to take the value statement to heart:

> *"Every organization needs values, but a lean organization needs them even more. When you strip away the support systems of staffs and layers, people have to change their habits and expectations, or else the stress will just overwhelm them."*[215]

In the 1992 corporate meeting in Boca Raton, Florida, Welch demonstrated that although the "flourish off" statement was taken out of the code, he had not forgotten it. It had been a spectacularly successful year for GE financially, and everyone was in a celebratory mood. Then Welch uttered one of his famous reality checks:

> *"Look around you: there are five fewer officers here than there were last year. One was fired for the numbers, four were fired for [lack of] values."*[216]

~

To ensure that managers are living up to GE values, they are rated by those they work for, those they work with, and those they supervise:

"To embed our values, we give our people 360-degree evaluations, with input from superiors, peers, subordinates. These are the roughest evaluations you can get, because people hear things about themselves they've never heard before."[217]

~

Even today, Welch says that a manager's people skills are as important as the profits he or she produces:

"Even senior people with good results, doing great jobs in terms of numbers but [who are] not walking the talk, have to be removed to support our values. We have to part company."[218]

FOUR TYPES OF LEADERS

In case the GE value statement did not get his message across, Welch continued to make his point:

"[W]hat we are doing is fragile. It's built on trust. The process can be set back in a heartbeat by people at any level who see leadership as a process of intimidation, people whose own lack of self-esteem makes them unable to trust and let go.

"To expect 284,000 people [1992 employment numbers] to deliver without the support, coaching, and encouragement of their leadership at every level is absurd. Understanding this, we have been taking a good long look—a look in the mirror if you will—at the various types of leadership we have in our company. We

put them into four categories, and I would guess they are pretty close to the same types you run into every day in business, schools, labs—in any institution."[219]

⌣

Welch sometimes ranks managers as As, Bs, and Cs. He says trying to turn C managers into As or Bs is a "wheel-spinning exercise." Push Cs out the door to B companies or C companies. GE is "an A-plus company" that can have its pick of the finest managers. "Shame on any of you who aren't facing up [to poor performers]. Move 'em out early," he instructed senior executives.[220]

⌣

Apparently, the A, B, and C concept refers to grades on performance. Welch talks about the four types of managers and how they fit in the GE culture:

Type I are people who not only deliver on performance commitments, but they believe in and promote GE's small-company values. "The trajectory of this group is onward and upward, and the men and women who comprise it will represent the core of our senior leadership into the next century."[221]

"Type I is everybody's star. These people deliver on commitments, financial or otherwise, and share our values. Values like a love of speed, a hatred of bureaucracy. Values like relishing change, not being paralyzed by it, and respecting everyone and engaging everyone in the cause of winning."[222]

Type II are just the opposite. They do not "meet commitments, nor share our values—nor last long at GE."[223] "They have to go," says Welch.[224]

~

Type III are more complicated, says Welch. They try hard, but "They miss some commitments, don't always make the numbers, but share all the values. They work well with people."[225]

Sometimes, they swing and miss:

> *"We encourage taking big swings, and Type III is typically given another chance."*[226]

~

Type IV are the real headaches: "This is the person who makes the numbers but forces them out of people rather than inspiring them to produce. This is your big shot, your tyrant, the person you'd love to be rid of—but oh those numbers."[227]

> *"Type IVs [deliver the goods] without regard to values, and in fact, often diminish them by grinding people down, squeezing them, stifling them. Some of these learned to change, most couldn't. The decision to begin removing Type IVs was a watershed—the ultimate test of our ability to 'walk the talk,' but it had to be done if we wanted GE people to be open, to speak up, to share, and to act boldly outside traditional 'lines of authority' and 'functional boxes' in this new learning, sharing environment."*[228]

Getting rid of Type IVs takes guts:

> *"We've been coming to grips with Type IV at GE because, while Type IV can give us the performance in the short term, he or she will never get the productivity and thus the performance we need for the long term. You can't take that level of performance from a workforce; they have to give it, not out of affection for management but because of the excitement and personal satisfaction that involvement in winning can provide them, and the security and rewards that can only come from winning."*[229]

~

John M. Trani, a former GE executive (apparently an A manager; he left GE to become CEO of Stanley Works) made this observation: "The Welch theory is those who do, get; those who don't, go."[230]

~ * ~

THE BEST MUTUAL FUND IN THE WORLD

GE has become a CEO "factory," supplying more top executives to American business than any other company. If you buy shares in the companies the GE alumni run, you may have "the best mutual fund in the world," says Steve Kerr, director of GE's Crotonville leadership training program.[231]

When Larry A. Bossidy was chosen chief executive of Allied-Signal Inc., the company's share price jumped 13 percent. When Stanley C. Gault assumed leadership at Goodyear Tire and Rubber, the share price immediately bumped up from $28 to $31. On the day in 1991 that Glen Hiner took over as head of Owens-Corning Fiberglas Corporation, the share price rose $2.25 to $23.25, and within a month, the shares were trading at $36.325. Every one of these stocks has steadily appreciated since. Each of these new CEOs had spent most of their careers at GE. Since Welch is likely to hold his job through the year 2000, talented GE executives who wanted to run their own show had little choice except to relocate.

Management Today claims, "Probably no single company has made such a singular contribution to the arts and wiles, the viewpoints and the techniques, of large-scale corporate management as GE."[232] Welch himself was earnestly courted by IBM before Louis V. Gerstner was hired as CEO in 1995.

Those executives who headed one of GE's businesses go to the next job with abundant experience. Many of GE's businesses qualify independently as Fortune 500 companies, and they are indeed operated as nearly independent entities.

"Ours is a company where there's a chance for [executives] to become general managers of a small business relatively early in their careers, and where they can grow that business and make it better than the best.[233]

There is, however, one important danger in hiring a GE-trained executive. During the 1980s, when Welch was restructuring GE, many executives were dismissed. Some were excellent employees who were merely in the wrong business or at the wrong level. Others, however, were subpar, the Type IV manager that Welch says has no future at GE. It behooves an executive search committee to know into which category a former GE-er fits.

Here are some CEOs, past and present, who cut their teeth at GE:

William Anders, General Dynamics

Norman P. Blake, Jr., USF&G

Larry A. Bossidy, Allied-Signal Inc.

Michael J. Emmi, Systems and Computer Technology

Stanley C. Gault, Rubbermaid Inc., and later,
    Goodyear Tire and Rubber Corp.

Fred Garry, late chief executive of Rohr Inc.

Robert Goldsmith, former chief executive, Rohr Inc.

Glen Hiner, Owens-Corning Fiberglas

Clyde Keaton, Clean Harbors

Chuck Lillis, MediaOne Group (Formerly U. S. West
    Media Group)

Michael Lockhart, General Signal Corp.

Daniel McGlaughlin, Equifax

Richard Miller, Wang Laboratories

George Schofield, Zurn Industries

Roger Shipke, Ryland Group Inc.

Harry C. Stonecipher, Sunstrand, and later,
    McDonnell Douglas Corp.

John M. Trani, Stanley Works

Walter Williams, Rubbermaid

Thomas Vanderslice, President of GTE, then CEO
    of Apollo Computer, and then CEO of M/A
    Com, which produces microwave components.

Alva O. Way, American Express Co.

WELCH, THE CHANGE AGENT

CHANGE BEFORE YOU HAVE TO

"There's a whole set of phrases that are designed to wait until disaster strikes. Phrases like: 'If it ain't broke, don't fix it,' or 'Don't be a solution in search of a problem,' or 'Don't break up a winning team.'

"We all use these over and over—a dismissal of someone trying to change something that's going just fine.

"But in truth, the wisdom may lie in changing the institution while it's still winning—reinvigorating a business, in fact, while it's making more money than anyone ever dreamed it could make."[234]

~

"We had constructed over the years a management apparatus that was right for its times, the toast of the business schools. Divisions, strategic business units, groups, sectors, all were designed to make meticulous, calculated decisions and move them smoothly forward and upward. This system pro-

duced highly polished work. It was right for the '70s . . .
a growing handicap in the early '80s . . . and would
have been a ticket to the boneyard in the '90s. So we
got rid of it . . . along with a lot of reports, meetings,
and the endless paper that flowed like lava from the
upper levels of the company."[235]

～

Welch says changing before a company is forced to do
so is about as easy as changing a tire while the car is
still going down the road. It's both risky and bound to
create controversy:

"No matter how many exciting programs you imple-
ment, there seems to be a need for people to spend
emotional energy criticizing the administration
of the programs rather than focusing on the sub-
stance."[236]

～

GE's greatest strength will be its adaptability:

"We want to be a company that is constantly renew-
ing itself, shedding the past, adapting to change."[237]

～

Welch tells GE-ers that there are two kinds of companies. One kind says the future will surprise us, but
we're not surprised to be surprised. The second type
is truly surprised, unprepared for the surprise, and
resistant to change. GE, he says, is the first kind of
company.[238]

～

"Managements that hang on to weakness for what-ever reason—tradition, sentiment, or their own man-agement weakness—won't be around in 1990."[239]

～

Welch initiated a two-phase revolution at GE. In the "hardware" phase, Welch restructured GE's basic businesses by selling, buying, and downsizing; and during the "software" phase, he shifted the corporate culture and employee mind-set.

"The decade of the 1980s imposed two distinct chal-lenges. In the first phase, through 1986, we had to pay attention to the 'hardware'—fixing the busi-nesses. In the second phase, from 1987 well into the 1990s, we've had to focus on the 'software.' Our sustained competitiveness can only come from improved productivity, and that requires the bottom-up initiatives of our people."[240]

～

The hardware changes—specifically, a shift toward the service sector—were wrenching for a company that from inception was engineering-oriented:

"It has been hard for the old equipment business, where building the latest high-efficiency this and high-efficiency that was the route to epaulets on your shoulder."[241]

～

The software changes were necessary to make the hardware changes work:

"A company can boost productivity by restructuring, removing bureaucracy, and downsizing, but it cannot sustain high-productivity growth without cultural change."[242]

~

"How do you bring people into the change process? Start with reality. Get all of the facts out. Give people the rationale for change, laying it out in the clearest, most dramatic terms. When everybody gets the same facts, they'll generally come to the same conclusion."[243]

~

Paradoxically, Welch says change must be consistent, persistent, and simply stated:

[Even at GE executive meetings, there is a] "relentless consistency, a pounding, a drumming, over and over. We don't change our mind. We don't jump around. We don't give them a new flavor of the month."[244]

~

"I'm in my 14th year of running a global company, and I've been wrong about a lot of things in those 14 years; but one prediction I've made at least 14 times that has always come true is that things are going to get tougher; the shakeouts more brutal and the pace of change more rapid."[245]

~

In this environment, he continues:

> *"[T]he difference between winning and losing will be how the men and women of our company view change as it comes at them. If they see it as a threat—as an ill wind to be resisted by keeping your head down and digging your feet in—we lose. But if they are provided the educational tools and are encouraged to use them—to the point where they see change as synonymous with opportunity, where they become receptive to it, even demand of it—then every door we must pass through to win big all around the world will swing open to us—new markets, exotic technologies, novel ventures, dramatic productivity growth."[246]*

~

While Welch preaches the value of change, he denies that he has changed:

> *"I haven't changed a thing! I try to adapt to the environment I'm in. In the '70s, when I was helping grow new businesses—at plastics, at medical—I was a wild-eyed growth boy. And then I got into the bureaucracy and I had to clean it out, so I was different in 1981. And now I'm in another environment. But that's not being 'born again.'*
>
> *"The ideas were always the same. We've been talking about reality, agility, ownership, and candor since the beginning. We just got it simpler and more carefully articulated over time."[247]*

Despite his protests, Gertrude G. Michelson, senior vice president of R. H. Macy & Co. and a GE director since 1976, says she has seen Welch mature:

> *"He has changed from competitive to cooperative, in the broadest sense—he understands that's the real top leadership role."*[248]

~

GE's corporate executive council meets four times a year at Crotonville to review policies and progress. Recently, the Lyceum, where the Corporate Executive Council meets, was remodeled. Steve Kerr says that when the top GE executives first gathered in the room—those who most ardently preach quick reaction to change—were confused and rattled. They shuffled around like they were playing musical chairs, momentarily befuddled because there was one less chair on the left side than there had been, and one more chair on the right. But, Kerr said, they figured it out reasonably quickly and took their seats.[249]

GO FOR THE LEAP

> *"Shun the incremental and go for the leap."*[250]

~

> *"Incremental change doesn't work very well in the type of transformation GE has gone through. If your change isn't big enough, revolutionary enough,*

the bureaucracy can beat you. Look at Winston Churchill and Franklin Roosevelt. They said, 'This is what it's going to be.' And then they did it. Big bold changes, forcefully articulated. When you get leaders who confuse popularity with leadership, who just nibble away at things, nothing changes. I think that's true in countries and in companies."[251]

~

"Most bureaucracies—and ours (at GE) is no exception—unfortunately still think in incremental terms rather than in terms of fundamental change. They think incrementally primarily because they think internally.

"Changing the culture—opening it up to quantum change—means constantly asking not how fast am I going, how well am I doing versus how well I did a year or two years before? [But] How fast and how well am I doing versus the world outside? Are we moving faster, and are we doing better against that external standard?"[252]

~

"How many textile companies died, going from north to south in search of marginally lower wage rates they thought would make them competitive— the incremental solutions—rather than coupling lower costs with a massive technological revitalization of the entire process?"[253]

~

GE learned about "bullet train thinking" from the CEO of Yokogawa, GE's Japanese partner in the medical systems business:

> *"He says if you want to increase the speed of the bullet train 10 mph, you add a little more horsepower. . . . But if you want to take it from 150 mph to 300 mph—double the speed of the bullet train—you've got to think about whether or not you widen the track, change the suspension system. You've got to think out of the box. It's not the same train with a little more tweak. It's a whole new thought."[254]*

The tools for making the bullet train change include boundaryless teams, stretch targets, best practices, and other GE concepts.

~

> *"The idea of faster pace—the quantum change—is not just reserved for entrepreneurs, for the fast, new start-up you hear about in Silicon Valley or Route 128 in Boston. It's not just reserved for skunk works. It's for everyone, everywhere."[255]*

MANAGING PARADOX

> *"What we need are leaders who understand the hidden realities, who understand the increasing number of paradoxes and linkages that confront us in business today that go beyond the simplicity of either-or."[256]*

~

"Effective leadership involves the acceptance and management of paradox. For example, we must function collectively as one company and individually as many businesses at the same time."[257]

〜

Welch says managers must play their own game well, but they won't last long unless they are team players:

"If you can't operate as a team player, no matter how valuable you've been, you really don't belong at GE."[258]

〜

Many business leaders may find it paradoxical that Welch, who is the devil himself when cutting costs, calls the budget process the "bane of corporate America." He explained it this way to former *Fortune* editor Marshall Loeb:

"Making a budget is an exercise in minimalization because everyone is always negotiating for the lowest number, not for the best result.

"If I worked for you, Marshall, you would come charging into the boardroom and say, 'I need four.' I would haggle all day, me making presentations with 50 charts, saying the right number is two. In the end, we'd settle on three. We'd go home and tell our families we had a helluva day at the office. And what did we do? We ended up minimizing our activity. We weren't dreaming, reaching. I was trying to get the lowest budget number I could sell you.

It's all backward. But if instead you ask people, 'give us all you can, give us your best shot at what you can do,' then you can't believe the numbers you'll get. You'll get more than you need. There's a trust built that people are going to give their best."[259]

PRODUCTIVITY: UNLIMITED JUICE IN THE LEMON

"Optimism, leadership, and productivity have been three of the characteristics that have moved this country to a special place in front of the nations of the world."[260]

∽

Everyone should understand the importance of productivity, according to Jack Welch. During the depths of the 1992 recession, he claimed the U.S. economy wasn't as woeful as many Americans believed it was:

∽

"Let me make the assumption for the moment that I've convinced you—and I recognize it as an assumption—that things aren't as bad as they seem, that there is plenty of opportunity for growth, that the glass is half full. The obvious question remains: How do you fill the glass to the brim?

"I'm convinced that the answer to that question lies in just one concept: Productivity—sustained productivity growth.

"If there is one thing that's for sure, it is the direct correlation between national productivity and national well-being.

"Look back at America of the '50s—the land of productivity. We had enormous pent-up demand, to be sure, but we also had productivity growth of 2.8 percent per year.

"It was that productivity that produced a 40 percent increase in real median family income over the decade of the '50s. College, vacation homes, second cars—things that had always been associated with the few—came within reach of the many, and at last within the aspirations of all."[261]

~

"Poor productivity can kill a century-old company in two to three years, and it can certainly change the relative standard of living of a two-century-old nation in less than a decade."[262]

~

Productivity, Welch says, can whip inflation. If inflation is 5 percent and productivity is 1 percent, a manager starts out four points behind last year's performance: "So what does the manager do? He immediately grabs the sales manager by the shirt and says, 'Get prices up.' He feels he has no choice—he has got to make his budget or there won't be any earnings. But what usually happens when he raises prices? He loses share. He's strangling! "But if he could gain 6 percent productivity, he'd start out ahead—despite inflation. The general manager can cut prices and gain share, or he can raise prices to increase profits. He is in control of his destiny."[263]

~

"Growing productivity must be the foundation of everything we do. We've been chasing it at GE for years. We once thought we could manage it into business operations, with control and hierarchies and vinyl books with charts. All we did was stifle people, sit on them, slow them up, and bore them to death. In the early '80s, we fell in love with robots and automation, and filled some of our factories with them as our employees looked on sullenly and fearfully. It didn't work.

"We now know where productivity—real and limitless productivity—comes from. It comes from challenged, empowered, excited, rewarded teams of people. It comes from engaging every single mind in the organization."[264]

~

"When a business becomes productive, it gains control of its destiny."[265]

GE's lighting business is a classic example. It was a mature, high-margin business that seemed to have topped out in the late 1980s. During the hardware revolution, it was one of the first GE companies to go global:

"Lighting, one of our oldest businesses, which less than five years ago had 21 percent of its sales outside the United States, today sells 38 percent in the non-U.S. global market."[266]

Yet lighting was a laggard in productivity. In 1986, John Opie, was put in charge and immediately did an analysis of every part of the business from manufacturing to packaging to distribution to incentive compensation. Within three years, lighting achieved the admirable productivity rate of 9 percent.

"[T]he highest growth is not coming from high-growth businesses like jet engines or plastics . . . where the conventional wisdom says it must come from . . . but instead from Mr. Edison's 114-year-old lighting business."[267]

~

When he first assumed leadership at GE, productivity rarely grew more than 1.5 percent annually. This compared with Japan's annual productivity growth rate of 8 percent:

"My obsession with the productivity issue is not based on academic research. Excuse a lapse into parochialism for a minute. GE started the '80s with GNP earnings growth because we had GNP productivity growth of 1 to 2 percent. As we doubled and then tripled productivity, we took off with 40 consecutive quarters of earnings growth in the '80s, with the big double-digit increases at the very end of the decade.

107

"Last year [1991] in the midst of this recession, we grew earnings per share 5 percent. We grew exports to $8.6 billion, up 21 percent from 1990, and our positive contribution to the U.S. balance of trade was $5.9 billion. Almost a billion dollars in Japan alone. Why? Advanced technology and stronger productivity were our big advantages."[268]

~

"Productivity is not the squeezing out of a rag. Productivity is the belief that there's an infinite capacity to improve anything."[269]

~

"America became more productive. It got more out for less in."[270]

~

And productivity growth isn't over yet, Welch insists:

"After 30 years of productivity growth, nobody in Japan asks, 'Is it over?' It's never over."[271]

~

"What we have done has barely scratched the surface. It turns out that there is, in fact, unlimited juice in that lemon. The fact is, this is not about squeezing anything at all: it is about tapping an ocean of creativity, passion, and energy that, as far as we can see, has no bottom and no shores."[272]

THE HARDWARE REVOLUTION

PUTTING MONEY ON THE RIGHT GAMBLES

When Welch became CEO in 1981, GE had 350 strategic businesses. Within months, he launched what was called GE's "hardware" revolution, a realignment of the shape, scope, and focus of the multinational corporation. Welch at first aimed at 15 core companies, then pared that to 14. He is now down to 11 core businesses operating in 50 different product and service lines ranging from lightbulbs to jet engines to financial services to television networks to sidewalk toilet kiosks.

~

On deciding which hardware investments GE should make:

> *"My biggest challenge will be to put enough money on the right gambles and to put no money on the wrong ones. But I don't want to sprinkle money over everything."*[273]

~

"In the 1970s and early 1980s, while the competitive invasion by Japanese companies hit many U.S. industries, GE chose its market battlegrounds very carefully, staying only in businesses where we held powerful competitive positions and technology edges, and exiting businesses such as consumer electronics where we did not."[274]

~

Welch began to think of three circles representing manufacturing, technology, and services, the three areas on which GE would concentrate. Then he set up another requirement:

"To the hundreds of businesses and product lines that made up the company we applied a single criterion: can they be number 1 or number 2 at whatever they do in the world marketplace? Of the 348 businesses or product lines that could not, we closed some and divested others. Their sale brought in almost $10 billion. We invested $18 billion in the ones that remained and further strengthened them with $17 billion worth of acquisitions.

"What remained [in 1989], aside from a few relatively small supporting operations, are 14 world-class businesses . . . all well positioned for the '90s . . . each one either first or second in the world market in which it participates."[275]

~

A Japanese publication criticized Welch for selling GE's television and other subsidiaries, calling it the "hollowing out" of American industry. He explained:

"GE's television business was ranked fifth, sixth, or seventh worldwide; Japanese manufacturers dominated the field. We had a medical business that was already number 1 globally. Its biggest competitor was Germany's Siemens. So we traded our losing television business to Thomson for their losing medical business, which would take us to number 2 in medical equipment in Europe. The medical venture there is now very profitable and makes us number 1 in the world by a larger margin.

"Whether or not GE has a television business has nothing to do with benefits or disadvantages for a country. It doesn't do anything for a country or its employees to be in weak businesses. Actually, the televisions are still being made in the United States. It doesn't matter who owns them."[276]

∾

"The businesses I eliminated were not simply in the red for two or three years; they had been depressed for 30 or 50 years in the long history of GE. And their employees had consciously become underdogs."[277]

∾

Welch downsized and discharged so many people that he was dubbed "Neutron Jack" after the bomb that kills people but leaves buildings standing. Welch feels he got a bum rap:

> *"Nuking somebody means you kill him. We start a renewal process. When people leave our company, we provide a soft landing. People who have been removed for not performing may be angry, but not one will say he wasn't treated with dignity. We can look ourselves in the mirror every morning and say we did what we could."*[278]

〜

Eventually, Welch accepted that the nickname had assumed mythic proportions and that he was stuck with it.[279]

〜

Because most workers believed they had lifetime employment at GE, the hardware changes came as a shock:

> *"The job security in those days was a given. Pretty solid. And so what we did, we're pretty proud of. We did some of the first soft landings in business. We gave six months notice for the first time; that wasn't mandated. We gave all kinds of benefits. My predecessor left me with a balance sheet that gave me the luxury to deal with this in a much better way than other companies that had to deal with it when they were going broke. So we were lucky. We had a healthy company that we were fixing."*[280]

~

Though the most dramatic part of the hardware revolution was over by 1985, Welch says it will never be finished:

"Restructuring is a road, not a destination."[281]

THREE BIG CIRCLES

Welch drew three strategic circles, each a focus of operation. In the first circle was core manufacturing, such as lighting and locomotives. In the second circle was technology-intensive businesses, and in the third circle was services. Each operation within its circle would be ranked first or second in its industry, or it would be eliminated.

"Anything outside the circles, we will fix, close, or sell."[282]

~

"I wanted to drive us into technologies and services, away from mundane manufacturing, if you will. So I developed a circle on services, technology, and manufacturing. And then I said—which was very controversial at the time—that we had to either fix, sell, or close. In 1981 or 1982 that was very controversial. In the 1990s, people are doing it every day. But at that time, it was very controversial, particularly for a large company.

"And out of that came a lot of—if you will—the [accusations of] harshness. What is this guy doing? Neutron Jack. Some of that stuff *developed out of that. But in the end, it was a way to articulate to a large crowd what we were going to do and what we were not going to do. And if you're outside the circles, people would say, 'What am I, in a leper colony? I joined GE and now I'm outside the circles?' So there was all this discussion about it. For me it was a vision. A way we were going to go. And it was back to being candid, facing reality. Reality: In those days, corporate America wasn't doing much of that.*

"I had it here in the company on a chart. I was sitting in a meeting like this in a room like this, and I grabbed a napkin, or whatever, and just drew it out, and a reporter took it [Forbes, 1984] *and drew it in a graphic. It turned out to be very helpful, actually—the little article and the fact that he did it—because it got widespread play. It was a whole new vision, new future, the article said. It was simple, visual, yet traumatic. If you weren't in the circles, it caused a real wrench to the organization."283*

~

"I find the three circles—core, high technology, and services—to be an easy way to explain our complex company, both internally and externally. They're helpful in developing appropriate resource allocations, and they certainly help maintain a long-term focus. The 15 businesses in these circles represent the

15 best chances for GE to have true world-leading businesses in 1990."[284]

NOTE: Eventually the 15 businesses were consolidated into 11.

The original group of businesses produced 90 percent of GE's earnings. They were:

Manufacturing: Construction equipment, lighting, major appliances, motor, transportation, and turbines.

High Technology: Aerospace, aircraft engines, industrial electronics, materials (plastics and engineered materials), and medical systems.

Services: Construction and engineering, financial services, information services, and nuclear services.

Three businesses outside the circle—GE Trading Company, Ladd Petroleum, and the Semiconductor Business Division—would never be world leaders, but they were considered critical to the success of those within the circles.

Those businesses designated as blatantly "outside" were housewares, central air conditioning, television and audio, cable, mobile, power delivery, and radio stations.

Only a few of GE's companies were first or second in their class at the time, among them lighting, power systems, and motors. Only plastics, gas turbines, and aircraft engines had strong international presence, and only gas turbines was a global leader.

It was Welch's goal to achieve market leadership, well-above-average returns on investment, and to leverage GE's existing strengths to the highest possible level.

> *"Linking technology to the marketplace and providing service offerings that are second to none will be the winning formula in all the [GE] circles."*[285]

> *"The three-circles concept is a way to visualize the company and the synergy between its parts, but it is not the way the company is actually organized. There is no executive vice president for each circle."*[286]

BE NUMBER 1 OR NUMBER 2— OR BE GONE

> *"There is no single grand plan for a company with as many businesses and markets as General Electric. But our strategic aim is to evolve into a company that's either number 1 or number 2 in its arenas."*[287]

> *"We made this decision based on our observation that when a number 1 market-share business entered a down cycle and sneezed, number 4 or 5 often caught galloping pneumonia."*[288]

~

In 1981, Welch gave a more detailed explanation to financial analysts:

"The winners in this slow-growth environment [of the 1980s] will be those who search out and participate in the real growth industries and insist upon being number 1 or number 2 in every business they are in—the number 1 or number 2 leanest, lowest-cost, worldwide producers of quality goods and services or those who have a clear technological edge, a clear advantage in a market niche."[289]

~

"Don't play with businesses that can't win. Businesses that are number 3, number 5 in their market—Christ couldn't fix those businesses. They're going to lose anyway."[290]

~

"It was a jarring concept [when introduced in 1981], but as the environment of the '80s grew increasingly intolerant of all but market leaders, number 1 or number 2 seemed more and more like mere common sense as company after company was forced to adopt it."[291]

~

Besides being a leader, GE had to be in the right game:

"Being number 1 or 2 in hula hoops would not do very much good."[292]

117

~

To be a leader in domestic markets is not enough. Globalization is essential:

> *"Our view as we entered the '80s focused, appropriately, on one powerful competitor: Japan, Inc. As we stand on the threshold of the '90s, we face not only an even more powerful Japan but a revitalized, confident Europe moving closer together and led by bold, aggressive entrepreneurs of the kind we simply didn't encounter in the '70s or early '80s. That huge Duke Power order that [GE's] Gas Turbine won, if bid 10 years ago probably would have been a domestic contest between GE and Westinghouse. To win it in 1989, we had to go to the mat with Asea/Brown Boveri, a Swedish-Swiss combination, Siemens of Germany, and a Westinghouse/Mitsubishi consortium."[293]*

~

Selling off the businesses that will never be number 1 or number 2 is like taking nasty medicine: sometimes you've got to do it to get healthy:

> *"Nothing's worse than the insecurities that result from hanging on to businesses that are weak in their marketplace, especially in nongrowing markets. No one is happy. They're not making money, they are not paying taxes, the employees come to work every day wondering whether it's their last day or not. There is a fear that stems from such insecurity that permeates the flesh."[294]*

118

Some observers accused Welch of limiting GE to first- or second-ranked businesses because he dislikes competition:

> *"Some people say I'm afraid to compete. I think one of the jobs of a businessperson is to get away from the slugfests and into niches where you can prevail. The fundamental goal is to get rid of weakness, to find a sheltered womb where no one can hurt you. There's no virtue in looking for a fight. If you're in a fight, your job is to win. But if you can't win, you've got to find a way out."[295]*

Welch said at the outset of the effort:

> *"I may be a babbling guy five years from now, sitting here mumbling, 'number 1, number 2,' but if it works internally, it will work, in time, externally."[296]*

FLATTENING THE GE WEDDING CAKE

General Electric's management structure was once described as an elaborate, many-layered wedding cake, becoming smaller as it went up. In 1985, Welch began what economist Joseph Schumpeter called "creative destruction." The hierarchical levels were trimmed from 29 to 6. When Welch was done, the structure looked more like a wagon wheel, laying flat on the ground. Top management was at the center and the rest of the company radiated out like the spokes of the wheel.

~

GE was delayered:

> *"During the '80s we eliminated layer after layer of management. We took down wall after wall separating functions. We reduced staff—the checkers, kibitzers. As we did this, we found, first at the business leadership level and then down in the organization, that people who were given space—trusted, allowed to make their own decisions—worked harder at making sure they made good decisions."*[297]

~

A critical step, one Welch says he postponed longer than he should have because the managers were good people and he liked them, was removing the sector executives:

> *"Simply by eliminating the company's top operating level, the sectors, we saved $40 million. But that was just a bonus that pales in importance to the sudden release of talent and energy that poured out after all the dampers, valves, and barriers of the sectors had been removed. We can say without hesitation that almost every single good thing that has happened within this company over the past few years can be traced to the liberation of some individual, some team, or some business."*[298]

~

"The way to get faster, more productive, and more competitive is to unleash the energy and intelligence and raw, ornery self-confidence of the American worker, who is still by far the most productive and innovative in the world.

"The way to harness the power of these people is not to protect them, not to sit on them, but to turn them loose, let them go, and get the management layers off their backs, the bureaucratic shackles off their feet, and the functional barriers out of their way."[299]

~

"Without all the din and prattle of bureaucracy, people listen as well as talk; and since there are fewer of them, they generally know and understand each other."[300]

~

Some GE-ers complained that, with half as many employees, they had twice as much to do:

"In reducing these layers we are trying to get the people in the organization to understand that they can't do everything they used to do. They have to set priorities. The less important tasks have to be left undone. Trying to do the same number of tasks with fewer people would be the antithesis of what we set out to achieve: a faster, more focused, more purposeful company."[301]

~

When asked about the so-called cement layer of middle management that stubbornly resists change, Welch said that cement can harden anywhere in a corporation:

> *"No level of management has a monopoly on cement, and to make middle management synonymous with a cement layer is a bad rap—and inaccurate."*[302]

~

On the other hand, delayering uncovered some problems with managers that Welch didn't even know about.

> *"What we found was that once you removed the layers, many managers were suddenly exposed who weren't leaders at all."*[303]

DOWNSIZING

The unavoidable consequence of restructuring and delayering is a smaller—a downsized—company. Welch believes GE's downsizing is actually rightsizing, and that he has done it responsibly:

> *"Closing a business or a plant is the most difficult part of a manager's job, one that no one wants, but a job that is unfortunately unavoidable in some situations."*[304]

Welch adds:

"We're trying to be lean and compassionate."[305]

~

"I hope that I am decisive, tough-minded, and all the other positive adjectives they use; someone who sets high standards, who is demanding, who wants General Electric to be the most competitive sustaining enterprise in American business. But I don't want anyone in GE to think that toughness for toughness sake, that macho or mean behavior, has any place in this company."[306]

~

"The cruelest thing any organization can do is not level with people. Then, too often, it's too late in careers, [and the company] must face problems that weren't dealt with when individuals had more options."[307]

~

Downsizing was especially painful at GE's nuclear power division. Not only did that business have to deal with corporate culture shock, it also suffered national disillusionment with nuclear power:

"Our people were the best and the brightest. They had given 30 years of their lives to nuclear power. When I said, in 1981, that there was not going to be another nuclear plant built in the United States, they were upset, they were angry, they were writing letters.

"Even today, if you ran a survey of nuclear, and asked, 'how do you like our strategy?' they'd say they don't like it. Not because of anything wrong with GE's strategy. They just don't like what's happened to their situation. They don't like reality. I feel for them. It's a tough deal. But the world decided nuclear power was not what it wanted."[308]

~

"The restructuring we did in the '80s was not without impact—on communities and on individuals. But because of our strong balance sheet, we were able to provide soft landings for those affected; and because we made the tough decisions early, we are here today stronger than ever."[309]

~ ✳ ~

HONEY, I SHRUNK GE

When Welch became chairman and chief executive officer at General Electric in 1981, the company had 440,000 employees worldwide. Gradually, the number shriveled:

1988: Welch's speech to shareholders: "This management system, designed to draw out the best in the 300,000 individuals who make up this company, *is* drawing it out."[310]

1991: Shareholder's meeting: "One of the privileges connected with my job is that I get to sit in this chair once a year and report the achievements of the 298,000 people who make up our company."[311]

1992: At a speech to business leaders in North Carolina, Welch said: "To expect 284,000 [GE] people to deliver without the support, coaching, and encouragement of their leadership at every level is absurd."[312]

1993: Shareholder's meeting: "We are determined to build a culture in General Electric where 200,000-plus people will come to work in search of a better way—every day."[313]

1996: By 1996, GE's employment figures seemed to stabilize at between 240,000 and 260,000.

NOTE: During his tenure at GE, Welch has made 509 acquisitions worth $53.2 billion and 310 dispositions worth $15.9 billion. There are no figures available on how many employees came and went with the various sales of divisions and purchases of others.

THE SOFTWARE
REVOLUTION

THE SOFT VALUES

By 1988, seven years after Welch took the helm at GE, the hardware, or structural changes were mostly in place. On a helicopter ride home after a session at Crotonville, Welch expressed his frustration and anger to James Baughman, then director of Crotonville. The company was not as innovative, open, changeable, adaptable, or creative as he wanted it to be. Soon, the second phase of the GE revolution was underway:

> *"In the first half of the 1980s, we restructured this company and changed its physical makeup. That was the easy part. In the last several years, our challenge has been to change ourselves, an infinitely more difficult task that frankly, not all of us in leadership positions are capable of."[314]*

Though Welch had first started talking about "soft values" in 1981, five years later, GE still wasn't operating under those principles. Philip Krantz, a former

GE employee who by then worked for Intel, wrote in a letter to *Fortune* magazine: "What I found was everything that Jack abhors. Instead of decisions being made by a liberated and empowered middle management, all decisions—save an individual's preference for lunch—were made by the unit's CEO. The spirited repartee in which Welch engages his executives to advantage by pushing the boundaries of their knowledge of, and commitment to a project, were instead viewed as personal affronts to authority.

"In my own business unit, attempts to ignite productivity by clearing the decks of mediocre (long tenured) performers were met with resistance at the top. Despite what was happening at corporate, at GECC change was not really viewed as either necessary or positive."[315]

~

Welch explained what he meant by soft values:

> *"I expect General Electric to significantly outpace the growth of the GNP. But I don't expect us to get there by setting a numerical target. I expect we will get there through soft values, like quality, like personal excellence, like commitment, like a creative ambience. All these things will meld together to give us a company that provides people with valued products and services that will permit us to grow faster than the GNP. Setting a numerical target won't make it happen."[316]*

~

"Silicon Valley and Route 128 were not only technological phenomena, they were people phenomena, and uniquely American. How well we approximate that type of creativity and fire in American companies will determine whether or not this nation wins in the '90s."[317]

〜

Len Schlesinger, a consultant hired to coach employees through "software" changes at GE says: "This is one of the biggest planned efforts to alter people's behavior since the Cultural Revolution."[318]

〜

It had to be big, Welch said:

"Without everybody embracing what we want to do, we haven't got a prayer."[319]

〜

One of the goals of the cultural revolution was to reduce workloads by eliminating all unnecessary tasks:

"If we end up with key people browbeaten, working 16 hours a day trying to get the same amount of data as before, then we haven't done it right."[320]

〜

Another goal was to change the interaction between labor and management:

"You know, all of a sudden 'manager' isn't the status word it has been for a century at GE. It has overtones of rear echelon—with the front lines consisting of people who run the machines, test the products, speak with the customers. We're learning a new reverence for what those people know."[321]

~

"We are betting everything on our people—empowering them, giving them resources, and getting out of their way."[322]

~

"Today, with advanced information systems and flat organizational structures, everyone has simultaneous access to the same information; everyone can be part of the game."[323]

~

"If we are to get the reflexes and speed we need, we've got to simplify and delegate more—simply, trust more. We need to drive self-confidence deep into the organization. A company can't distribute self-confidence, but it can foster it by removing layers and giving people a chance to win. We have to undo a 100-year old concept and convince managers that their role is not to control people and stay 'on top' of things, but rather to guide, energize, and excite."[324]

~

Not only was GE ready for softer values, so was the whole country:

> *"You've got to be hard to be soft. You have to demonstrate the ability to make the hard, tough decisions—closing plants, divesting, delayering—if you want to have any credibility when you try to promote soft values. We reduced employment and cut the bureaucracy and picked up some unpleasant nicknames, but when we spoke of soft values— things like candor, fairness, facing reality—people listened."[325]*

WORKOUT

Central to the cultural revolution at GE was a process called "workout." In 1988, a team of consultants was assembled to figure out a process. The first GE workout session took place in March 1989.

The idea was to hold a three-day, informal town meeting with 40 to 100 employees from all ranks of GE. The boss kicked things off by reviewing the business and laying out the agenda, then he or she left. The employees broke into groups, and aided by a facilitator, attacked separate parts of the problem. At the end, the boss returned to hear the proposed solutions. The boss had only three options: The idea could be accepted on the spot; rejected on the spot; or more information could be requested. If the boss asked for more information, he had to name a team and set a deadline for making a decision.

At first, GE employees hesitated to speak out, and some managers were reluctant to let them solve problems. But it caught on, and workout sessions became freewheeling and intense. Eventually, the workout process became less formal and spread throughout the company.

> *"Workout was nothing more complicated than bringing people of all ranks and functions—managers, secretaries, engineers, line workers, and sometimes customers and suppliers—together into a room to focus on a problem or an opportunity, and then acting rapidly and decisively on the best ideas developed, regardless of their source."*[326]

~

> *"At these workout sessions, all the things that people used to mutter about around the water cooler on the weekends were finally brought up openly, and in many cases, resolved on the spot. These meetings are predicated on a belief that the people closest to the work know it best and are best qualified to make it better."*[327]

~

Workout had four primary goals:
1. To build trust.
2. To empower employees.
3. To eliminate unnecessary work.
4. To create a new paradigm for GE, that of a boundaryless organization.

~

Workout had five steps:

Step 1. Link weak performance to unproductive work practices.

Step 2. Engage coworkers in the workout process.

Step 3. Review inefficient procedures and practices.

Step 4. Functional groups reach consensus on suggested changes.

Step 5. Present recommendations to boss and get the boss to either agree, reject, or assign responsibility for further study.

~

Dr. Steve Kerr was on the team that developed workout. He says that when a boss has agreed to implement a suggestion: "Every recommendation has to have a champion, someone in the room, even if it's the newest hire or lowest clerk. It is his job to get it done. Every recommendation also has to have a roadblock-buster, a high-level person who will remove roadblocks."

The roadblock buster gives the champion his or her telephone number, pager number, or some way to get in touch directly, at any time. If a roadblock is thrown up in the workplace, the executive must arrange to have it removed.[328]

~

Workout evolved its own language. *Low-hanging fruit* are problems that are easily solved. *Rattlers* are problems that are easy to recognize because they make a lot of noise. *Pythons* represent problems that are hidden and entwined in bureaucracy. Pythons can put up a good fight.

~

Bill DiMaio, a team leader for the combuster shops at GE's aircraft manufacturing unit in Lynn, Massachusetts, described the workout experience this way: "Sometimes, as a manager at a workout, you feel foolish, like, 'why didn't I listen to this before?' Some people have this perception, 'gee, if I sit on the hot seat and if I'm insecure about taking someone else's idea, instead of coming from me, it's going to look like I don't know what I'm doing.' You have to get over this mind-set. I never felt intimidated; I always felt invigorated." While there are some "dog" ideas, DiMaio says that 95 percent of the recommendations are good ones.[329]

~

Welch describes workout as:

> *"A relentless, endless companywide search for a better way to do everything we do."*[330]

~

> *"[W]e like to say 'workout blew up the building.' Consider a building: It has walls and floors; the*

walls divide the functions, the floors separate the levels. Workout took out the walls and floors, leaving all the bodies in one big room."[331]

~

The payoff, if workout succeeded, Welch said, would be enormous:

"We'll have a company that is fueled by, that runs on, the unique attributes that we know exist in the American spirit—irreverence, curiosity, individualism, intellectual ferment; a company where jargon and double-talk and bureaucracy are ridiculed, and candor is demanded. We're not going to get a company like that by reading how-to books and trying to imitate other cultures."[332]

~

At his first workout session, one middle-aged employee confirmed that GE was on the right path: "For 25 years," the employee said, "you've paid for my hands when you could have had my brains as well—for nothing."[333]

~

"I see workout as a vehicle that, if totally and passionately implemented, will get us eventually to the speed, simplicity, and self-confidence we need to have to win against what's ahead in the '90s and beyond."[334]

~

SIMPLICITY

Welch focuses on three concepts that give GE enormous energy:

"Speed, simplicity, and self-confidence. We've been characterized over the years as the 'best-managed' company, the 'financial wizards,' or other labels. If we are to be the clear winners we must be in the '90s, we will need to become the fastest, simplest, and most self-confident company on Earth."[335]

~

"Simplicity is a quality sneered at today in cultures that like their business concepts the way they like their wine, full of nuance, subtlety, complexity, hints of this and that. In the '90s, cultures like that will produce sophisticated decisions loaded with nuance and complexity that arrive at the station long after the train has gone."[336]

~

"You can't believe how hard it is for people to be simple, how much they fear being simple. They worry that if they're simple, people will think they're simpleminded. In reality, of course, it's just the reverse. Clear, tough-minded people are the most simple."[337]

~

"At GE, we're driving to be lean and agile, to move faster, to pare away bureaucracy. We're subjecting

every activity, every function, to the most rigorous review, distinguishing between those things which we absolutely need to do and know versus those which would be merely nice to know."[338]

~

To simplify the business environment and focus his managers' thinking, Welch asks them to prepare one-page answers to five strategic questions:

1. What does your global competition look like over the next several years?
2. What have your competitors done in the last three years to upset those global dynamics?
3. What have you done to them in the last three years to affect those dynamics?
4. How might your competitor attack you in the future?
5. What are your plans to leapfrog the competition?[339]

~

"In our major appliance business in Louisville a few years ago, people on the assembly line suddenly found two levers in front of them. One lever stopped the line. The other sent a part on its way only *after an individual was satisfied that it was perfect. The line workers suddenly became the final authority on the quality of their work. The cynics scoffed when this system was proposed, predicting chaos or pro-*

duction at a snail's pace. What happened? Quality
increased enormously and the line ran faster and
smoother than ever."[340]

～

Simplicity, as Welch points out, isn't always so simple
to accomplish. Take process mapping, for example.
GE employees work with complex and sophisticated
technologies. Management soon learned that to
simplify, they had to have an exact picture of the
process.

A process map is a manufacturing flowchart that
shows every step, no matter how small, in making an
item. Managers, workers, suppliers, and customers
work on the map together, putting diamonds here,
circles or squares there to indicate the type of action
that has occurred. The process map for GE's turbine
engine took more than a month to complete and
stretched completely around a large conference room.
But when the map was done, employees knew pre-
cisely what was happening and could more easily see
where steps could be eliminated, combined, or moved
elsewhere for greater speed and efficiency.

～

"Simplicity is absolutely essential to getting the envi-
ronment, the vision, the plan across to large groups
of people at all levels, both inside and outside the
company."[341]

～

"Complexity slows and saps everything it touches—except the bureaucracy. Bureaucracies crave it. Frightened bureaucrats love it. I hate bureaucracy. I see what it does to people."[342]

SPEED

Welch insists that only speedy companies will survive:

"The '90s will make the '80s look like a walk in the park. We face a decade that is orders of magnitude greater in difficulty than anything we've seen before. The Japanese are more competitive at home, they are buying American companies outright and building plants in Europe. Europeans are facing us with new vigor in every business. Practically every power systems order in the United States is in a struggle against three or four European and Japanese players, when only a few years ago it would have been GE versus Westinghouse. Korea and Taiwan were pretty much sourcing centers just a few years ago. Now they are world-class international players. The bottom line is that change will be more rapid than we've seen in the past—and we must become faster."[343]

∼

"We have to get faster if we are to win in a world where nothing is predictable except the increasingly rapid pace of change.

"When we met with our shareowners last April [1990] we were marveling at the convulsions in

Eastern Europe, the fall of the Berlin Wall, and the turmoil in the Soviet Union. But Saddam Hussein's name never came up in the conversation. Less than six months later, the events in Europe, which people had been describing as the most significant in half a century, were shoved off the screen as the invasion of Kuwait, the war, and the victory took center stage.

"So while we cannot possibly know what events will transform our world by April of next year, we do know that we have to become faster in anticipating and reacting to them."[344]

～

"Today's global environment, with its virtually real-time information exchanges, demands that an institution embrace speed. Faster, in almost every case, is better."[345]

～

"Speed is everything. It is the indispensable ingredient in competitiveness. Speed keeps businesses—and people—young. It's addictive, and it's a profoundly American taste we need to cultivate."[346]

～

Speed and simplicity go together, said Welch:

"Simple messages travel faster, simpler designs reach the market faster, and the elimination of clutter allows faster decision making."[347]

～

Speed is critical to new product introduction, says Welch.

"Market windows open and shut faster than ever. Product life cycles that were once measured in years now typically last for months—even weeks."[348]

~

In order to move products rapidly from the laboratory to markets, Welch said:

"I want to see high-level managers in the labs, shaking chemists by the shirt."[349]

~

When asked by a *Business Week* reporter how he felt about complaints that GE put pressure on suppliers to make things quicker, deliver them faster, and with fewer defects, Welch replied:

"I'm not embarrassed to say: 'Put pressure on them.' I'm not timid about that. All these small companies that serve us, the machine shops around all of our plants, are gone if we lose the competitive business. If we got out of the turbine business in Schenectady, [it's] lights out for all the entrepreneurs that have done so wonderfully serving us."[350]

~

Welch says that he needs to be as quick to change as anyone else.

"I remember when The Wall Street Journal *went from two sections to three. I was so traumatized for*

48 hours. Where to find things! When you think about it, these things do change us. And we've got to just keep talking about it. When I'm at Crotonville, that's all I talk about—change, change, change. Be ready for it, see it, anticipate it, be ahead of it, create it. Don't sit still. Anybody sitting still, you can guarantee they're going to get their legs knocked out from under them."[351]

~

Indeed, Welch and his team have become champions at clinching the quick deal. It took just three days in 1989 to seal an alliance with the British company GEC. NBC took one weekend to win the exclusive rights to broadcast the Olympics until 2008, at a cost of $4 billion.

SELF-CONFIDENCE

GE must build self-confidence in its employees, Welch says:

"[J]ust as surely as speed flows from simplicity, simplicity is grounded in self-confidence. Self-confidence does not grow in someone who is just another appendage on the bureaucracy . . . whose authority rests on the bureaucracy . . . whose authority rests on little more than a title . . . people who are freed from the confines of their box on the organization chart, whose status rests on real-world achievement . . . those are the people who develop self-confidence to be simple,

to share every bit of information available to them, to listen to those above, below, and around them, and then move boldly."[352]

～

Welch says he wants GE management to have: ". . . the confidence to lead and the confidence to share."[353]

～

"The horizontal barriers between corporate functions grow because a worker's sense of security is built on knowing and protecting his place in the bureaucracy. Workers lose sight of the overall goals of the company:

"How do you change a mind-set that is more than a century old?

"We know the answer—the antidote—because we saw it at work, at least in pockets, during the '80s. It's self-confidence. Give people the chance to make a contribution to winning, let them gain the self-confidence that comes from knowing their role in it, and before long they abandon the paraphernalia of status and bureaucracy. They simply don't need it anymore.

"Self-confidence is the fuel of productivity and creativity, decisiveness, and speed."[354]

～

Self-confidence, Welch figures, accounts for the way GE's Transportation Systems (mainly locomotives) and Industrial Power Systems (turbines) pulled back from a precipice when management discovered it timed markets inaccurately. Transportation Systems had introduced a low cost, higher technology new locomotive just as the railroad market took a dive. Welch says both divisions saw the error of their ways early and had the self-confidence to change by themselves:

> *"Both went through purgatory in the 1980s, in the bottom of market troughs of several years' duration that saw few orders in locomotives and none in large steam turbines."[355]*
>
> *"Instead of closing or selling these businesses, we reduced their costs consistent with the market, invested to make them more competitive ($300 million in locomotives alone), and stuck with them through the lean years—not out of sentimentality or inertia but because they are large, world-leading businesses with big potential and because doing so fits our strategy. And, in 1988, we saw a significant market revival under way in locomotives and the approaching dawn of a revival in areas of the turbine business."[356]*

∼

With self-confidence comes ownership, Welch says:

> *"[O]wnership means having the freedom to take advantage of an opportunity, to move quickly before being told what to do. When people take ownership at any level in the organization, the freedom to act*

brings with it the responsibility to manage the impact of their actions—on corporate earnings, on corporate reputation, on quality, and the long-term health of the company. I hope ownership creates an environment where self-initiative is expected, where individuals are willing to bring up ideas, to challenge the status quo.

"If this ownership concept means people reaching, speaking out, then managers at every level will be forced to deal with adjusting the pace. We'll be able to work with the accelerator and the brake, rather than worry whether there's enough gas in the tank."[357]

～

There is a time when it's dangerous to be overly self-confident, Welch warns. That time is when a business is doing extremely well:

"Managing success is a tough job. There's a very fine line between self-confidence and arrogance. Success often breeds both, along with a reluctance to change."[358]

～

"Managing in a difficult environment trains you a hell of a lot better than riding the wave of success. When the ship is going down, everyone knows to get out the lifeboats."[359]

LABOR UNIONS

Though GE has not had a nationwide strike since 1969, the labor unions representing 38,500 GE workers have sometimes been harsh critics. And when labor negotiations begin in 1997, Welch came out swinging.

In his January, 1997 comments to management, among other things, Welch stated his position on pending negotiations. Edward L. Fire, president of the International Union of Electrical Workers, requested that GE remain neutral during recruitment drives in nonunion GE facilities. Additionally, Fire said he would seek job security provisions for GE workers similar to those won by United Auto Workers in Detroit in 1996.

In a fiery speech, Welch insisted that those and other union demands were "not for us in any way." He then added, "You better get prepared like you've never been prepared...to operate in a strike and not flinch."[360]

Welch's message was clear: "We don't need some third party to give people voice."[361]

Business Week reported that Fire was furious at Welch's remarks and shot off a letter saying so. "Welch made a serious mistake talking like that," Fire wrote.[362]

When a contract was signed with the International Union of Electronic Workers and United Electrical Workers in July 1997, the union lost a few points, but they also got a lot, including a 13 percent pay increase over three years, an extra holiday, job retraining, early retirement, and rehiring provisions.

Despite the tension, Welch says he understands why workers unionize:

> "There's always going to be a need for a voice for employees. And where they don't get it from the management and the company, they will have to get it through an organization. And unfortunately, there's always some situation somewhere that some leader or some boss or some thing creates an event [in which] employees don't feel they were treated fairly. And they don't get voice and dignity. I tell our people at every class at Crotonville: 'Your job is to give voice and dignity to people. It is absolutely the critical thing. You don't have to take their voice and do exactly what they want, but you have to listen. You have to give them dignity that their voice counts.' That's why this, 'ideas are accepted from any level,' is a big deal. Because the quality of an idea is what counts. And that people have voice and feel they have a place to vent, tell their story, the need for organization naturally goes down.
>
> "My father was a product of the union movement. And thank God he was in it. His good wages got me to school and other things. That was an era. It was different. So times changed. There is more enlightenment, information is more important. I told a fellow in Evendale, Ohio, who asked me, 'What about jobs for my son?' 'Will my son be able to have my job?' I said I can't guarantee that. I don't know that. What I'd be sure I'd do if I were you, I'd be sure I'm working to get him to college. I'd get him as globally sophisticated as I could. I'd get him steeped in information technology, because then I'd know he'd have a job. Whether

146

he can do your job 20 years from now, I don't know that. I don't know that turning that lathe will be there. I hope it is. But I can't guarantee it. I guarantee an education and a global instinct will give him a great career."[363]

~

"Increased job security and increased job satisfaction will come to those businesses that understand their competitive world, deal with it, and win in it."[364]

~

Welch says he hopes GE will offer both financial rewards and spiritual rewards to employees:

"It's been said that most people's jobs are too small for their spirits. I want a company where every single job grows to the size of its owner's spirit."[365]

~ * ~

A BOUNDARYLESS GE

It isn't enough that General Electric moves with ease across national borders; Welch wants to eliminate all boundaries that limit the ability of workers to do their jobs:

"Our dream for the 1990s is a boundaryless company, a company where we knock down the walls that separate us from each other on the inside and from our key constituencies on the outside. The boundaryless company we envision will remove the barriers among engineering, manufacturing, mar-

*keting, sales, and customer service; it will recognize
no distinction between domestic and foreign operations—we'll be as comfortable doing business in
Budapest and Seoul as we are in Louisville and
Schenectady. A boundaryless organization will
ignore or erase group labels such as 'management,'
'salaried,' or 'hourly,' which get in the way of people
working together. A boundaryless company will
level its external walls as well, reaching out to key
suppliers to make them part of a single process in
which they and we join hands and intellects in a
common purpose—satisfying customers."[366]*

~

Welch knows that "boundaryless" is not a graceful
word. Yet it conveys the message:

*"In designing a high-performance airplane, engi-
neers work incessantly at eliminating or flattening
any protruding surfaces that produce drag. The
result is a clean design that moves quickly and
smoothly through the air. In a company, the drag
comes from boundaries, the walls that grow between
functions such as finance and marketing and manufacturing, boundaries between suppliers and the
company, between the company and customers.
Each of these boundaries is a speed bump that slows
the enterprises. Each piece of turf within these
boundary walls is defended by the watchdogs of
bureaucracy. The process of getting through function after function can be so time-consuming and*

complex that it can force the organization to focus on itself, on its own inner workings, and distract it from its real mission: serving customers."[367]

～

"Picture a building. Companies all added floors as they got bigger. Size adds floors. Complexity adds walls. We all build departments—transportation departments, research departments. That's complexity. That's walls. The job all of us have in business is to flatten the building and break down the walls. If we do that, we will be getting more people coming up with more ideas for the action items that a business needs to work with."[368]

～

"Boundaryless behavior laughs at the concept of little kingdoms called finance, engineering, manufacturing, and marketing, sending each other specs and memos, and instead gets them all together in a room to wrestle with issues as a team."[369]

～

"Boundaryless behavior evaluates ideas based on their merit, not on the rank of the person who came up with them. It assumes that there isn't a customer in the world who doesn't have something valuable to share with you, so why not hand them a coffee mug and bring them into the room when you sit down to design a new product?"[370]

～

The old GE prejudice against anything NIH (not invented here) had to go:

"This boundaryless learning culture killed any view that assumed the 'GE way' was the only way or even the best way. The operative assumption today is that someone, somewhere, has a better idea; and the operative compulsion is to find out who has that better idea, learn it, and put it into action—fast."[371]

~

An example of how a boundaryless GE works:

"Our medical systems business, for instance, is a world leader in remote diagnostics, which means an installed GE CT scanner can be remotely monitored by our service people as it operates in a hospital. They can detect and repair an impending malfunction, sometimes online, sometimes before the customer even perceives there is a problem. Medical systems has shared this technology with our jet engine business, with locomotives, with motors and industrial systems, and with power systems, enabling them to monitor the performance of jet engines in flight, of locomotives pulling freight, of running paper mills, and of turbines in operation in customer power plants."[372]

~

The GE medical systems maintenance center in Buc, near Versailles, France, monitors equipment worldwide by satellite and often is able to make repairs by remote control. A computer center in Florence, Italy, checks 11,000 GE turbines operating everywhere from Siberia to Chile, and tries to service the equipment before a breakdown occurs. Some experts say Welch has taken GE through three phases: restructuring, globalization, and now, a move to become a service-oriented company. Welch insists that GE will stay in manufacturing, since all of its services are either linked to or support GE's own products.

～

"Our job is to sell more than just the box."[373]

～

Welch says people everywhere prefer a boundaryless environment:

"People want to be boundaryless in any culture. In Hungary, at our Tungsram facility, we've got 11 plants sharing 'best practices.' The energy is enormous. We're bringing the team from there to our lighting plants in the United States to show them some of the 'work-out' techniques they've used there to improve cycle time and processes. So, in every plant we have in every country, people are the same. They want to be more involved. No one wants to be in a box, to be locked in."[374]

～

Peggy Quinn Neimer, a GE attorney, says the philosophy of boundarylessness could benefit women employees: "I feel that GE's attempt to become boundaryless represents a great opportunity for women, because boundaries have traditionally functioned to keep women out."[375]

~

"Boundaryless is the language, the behavior definer, the culture, the soul of a true global enterprise. It ignores geography, borders, accents, currencies, and unites people of all cultures."[376]

SEARCHING THE PLANET FOR THE BEST PRACTICES

GE has, since Edison, been a fountainhead for bright ideas. Why look anywhere else for a better way? GE-ers believed that if it was NIH (not invented here), a product or procedure had little merit. Once GE started examining everything it did, it became clear that no one individual or single company owned all the good ideas. A worldwide search began for "best practices," Welch says:

"GE began to systematically roam the world, learning better ways of doing things from the world's best companies."[377]

~

"Our behavior is driven by a fundamental core belief: the desire, and the ability, of an organization to continuously learn from any source, anywhere;

152

and to rapidly convert this learning into action is its ultimate competitive advantage."[378]

~

"In Louisville recently, we needed a new transmission for a washing machine—a part we have traditionally designed ourselves and sourced from an outside supplier. This time, rather than start a GE engineering team wrestling with the design of the transmission, we went instead to four qualified suppliers whose businesses are focused on components like this, and asked them to give us their best shot on a new design; and they did. The result is, we are getting a better transmission than we could have designed ourselves, and we're getting it faster and at lower cost, because we had four times more brains focused on the problem than we would have had if we had done it the traditional way and stayed behind the horizontal boundary we had created between us and the outside."[379]

~

Some "best practices" have come from Wal-Mart, a company that Welch admires:

"Wal-Mart, in my opinion, clearly made a connection between the customer and every employee in Wal-Mart. And they work on that every single day. They just can't stand not filling a customer need. If they're out of blankets in Minneapolis, they've got a

153

computer system that will move the blankets instan-
taneously to Minneapolis. Or if their antifreeze is
low in Chicago and high in Kalamazoo, they'll move
it. An insatiable desire to make customers love 'em.
And tying their personal rewards over the years to
doing that, they've seen enormous wealth created at
all levels of the store."[380]

~

When he says "best practice," Welch means the best:

"[T]he only ideas that count are the A ideas. There
is no second place. That means we have to get every-
one in the organization involved. If you do that
right, the best ideas will rise to the top."[381]

~

"We don't claim to be the global fountainhead of
management thought, but we may be the world's
thirstiest pursuer of big ideas—from whatever their
source—and we're not shy about adopting and adapt-
ing them."[382]

~

"[W]e never shut up about the great things that lie
ahead for a company whose people get up every
morning and come to work knowing—convinced—
that there is a better way of doing everything they
do, and determined to find out who knows that
way and how they can learn it."[383]

TEAMWORK

Teamwork has become easier since GE's software revolution:

> *"The quest to make GE the most exciting and successful enterprise on Earth in this decade will be won on the factory floor, in the office, in the field, face to face with customers, with everyone understanding and focused on the essential mission of a corporation: serving customers."*[384]

Welch draws upon his own experience when trying to build team spirit:

> *"I remember getting a phone call from some financial guy in Fairfield when I was running plastics. He told me I had to give up $60 million of capital spending that was already approved. Why, why? The answer was that the XYZ division needed the money more than I did. So you wound up hating the other businesses, and competing against them, instead of working with them."*

Today, that is different:

> *"When appliances had their [refrigerator] compressor problem, guys from the other businesses saw that Roger Schipke was a victim of bad luck and began volunteering help—chipping in $20 million here, $10 million there, and so on."*[385]

One of the strengths of GE's quality improvement program is that it builds teams that encompass both customers and suppliers:

> *"I was in London at the beginning of June [1997]. The president of the GE mortgage company came in with his team and two customers. He was a black belt in Six Sigma quality. He talked about process, about cutting the time from this to this. His customer talked about how the customer had gained share through his efforts. He also showed his profitability in front of the customer. The relationship . . . it was a snapshot into GE of the next century."*[386]

STRETCH

To Welch, there is a big difference between pushing employees too hard and letting them set high goals for themselves that require extra imagination, brains, and skill to achieve:

> *"What we call 'stretch' simply means figuring out performance targets, from profitability to new product introductions, that are do-able, reasonable, and within our capabilities, and then raising our sights higher—much higher—toward goals that at the outset seem to require superhuman effort to achieve. We have found that by reaching for what appears to be the impossible, we often actually do the impossible; and even when we don't quite make it, we inevitably wind up doing much better than we would have done."*[387]

"A stretch atmosphere replaces a grim, heads-down determination to be as good as you have to be, and asks instead, how good can you be?"[388]

"Stretch means that we all try for huge gains while having no idea how to get there: but our people figure out ways to get there. I was in Japan in the fall and I saw Toshiba's new VCR. They had a stretch goal: produce it with half the parts, in half the time, at half the cost. They sent a team away to design the new model and ended up reducing the number of parts by 60 percent and producing it in one year instead of the usual two."[389]

Though workers at GE often hit stretch targets, they sometimes fall short. GE set two stretch goals for 1995: to achieve 10 inventory turns in the year, and to achieve a 15 percent operating margin. Those were ambitious goals, since the company had never reached five turns and barely achieved an 11 percent operating margin. That year, the company made only nine turns, one short of the target, but it did hit a 15 percent operating margin. Even the failed goal represented a big improvement over past performance.

"In GE today, this is not a 'miss,' or a 'broken commitment,' or a 'black eye,' but a triumph to be celebrated,

an achievement that is providing the cash to finance the acquisitions we want and a stock buy-back."[390]

~

"Because this [GE] management team has been together for a long time, trust has grown, and trust is an indispensable ingredient that allows a business to set big stretch targets. GE business leaders do not walk around all year regretting the albatross of an impossible number they hung around their own necks. At the end of the year, the business is measured, not on whether it hit the stretch target, but on how well it did against the prior year, given the circumstances.

"An exciting by-product of stretch behavior is the enormous surge of self-confidence that has grown across our company as people see themselves achieving things they once suspected were beyond them."[391]

~

Welch believes people stretch better when they are reaching for something they want. GE expanded its stock option bonus program from about 400 people in the 1980s to 22,000 by 1996.

~

"I've rewarded failures by giving out awards to people when they've failed, because they took a swing. Keep taking swings. I teach a course at Crotonville for six hours—four to six hours—on leadership. I always say, if the chairman can buy

Kidder Peabody and mess it up, you can do about anything. It was on the front page of The Wall Street Journal *19 times. Now, if the chairman can do that and still survive, you ought to be able to take swings everywhere. You can hardly do worse.*"[392]

~

"Punishing failure assures that no one dares."[393]

~

"Stretch can only occur in an environment where everyone is totally committed to a rigid set of core values— integrity, trust, quality, boundaryless behavior—and to outperforming every one of our global competitors in every market environment."[394]

~

Think big, Welch says:

"Decimal points are for bureaucrats."[395]

~

"I hope you won't think I'm being melodramatic if I say that the institution ought to stretch itself out, to reach to the point where it almost comes unglued."[396]

SIX SIGMA QUALITY

"Quality means literally providing something that's better than the best, not just better than most."[397]

159

During the early 1980s, when GE restructured its hardware to compete against foreign competitors, Welch says that companies such as Motorola, Texas Instruments, Hewlett-Packard, and Xerox did not have the same luxury. The only competitive edge they had was the quality of their products. Consequently, these companies became experts on quality control and improvement. In a survey of employees, GE learned that most workers wanted to improve their own quality, and believed it could be done. With the help of consultant Mikel Harry of the Six Sigma Academy in Scottsdale, Arizona, GE turned its attention to quality control. Six Sigma became Welch's passion for the late 1990s.

NOTE: Sigma is the term statisticians use when measuring standard deviation.

∽

"We have a massive scientifically based quality undertaking in progress at GE, which will take us, within four years, to a level of process excellence that will produce fewer than four defects per million operations performed in every manufacturing and service process across the company. It is the most challenging and potentially rewarding initiative we have ever undertaken at General Electric."[398]

∽

At GE's 1996 annual meeting in Charlottesville, Virginia, Welch explained what Six Sigma means:

"A typical process at GE generates about 35,000 defects per million, which sounds like a lot, and is a lot, but it is consistent with the defect levels of most successful companies. That number of defects per million is referred to in the very precise jargon of statistics as about three and one-half sigma. For those of you who flew to Charlottesville, you are sitting here in your seats today because the airlines' record in getting passengers safely from one place to another is even better than six sigma, with less than one-half failure per million.

"If you think about airlines, they run two operations. They get you from point A to point B from seven to eight sigma. Your bags get there at three sigma."[399]

~

Only a handful of companies in the world, several in Japan and Motorola in the United States, have achieved a Six Sigma level of quality.

~

GE had quality control programs previously, but they did not permeate the company the way Six Sigma does.

"We blew up the old quality organization, because they were off to the side. Now, it's the job of the leader, the job of the manager, the job of the employee—everyone's job is quality."[400]

~

> *"It has been remarked that we are just a bit 'unbalanced' on the subject [of Six Sigma]. That's a fair comment. We are."*[401]

Welch knows the high cost of low-quality products. In 1981, GE's dishwasher line lost 18 percent of its market share from the previous year, and washing machines lost 16 percent of their market share because GE's products were not of competitive quality. Welch acknowledged that consumer confidence, once gone, is not easily regained:

> *"A consumer punch in the eye does not go away for maybe a decade."*[402]

∿

> *"We want to change the competitive landscape by being not just better than our competitors, but by taking quality to a whole new level. We want to make our quality so special, so valuable to our customers, so important to their success, that our products become their only real value choice."*[403]

∿

Six Sigma was launched in late 1995 with 200 projects. By 1997, it involved more than 6,000 projects. GE has spent about $500 million so far, but expects to save some $500 to $600 million in 1997 alone.

> *"Forty percent of every manager's bonus is tied to his or her progress on quality results. Quality is the top item on every agenda in every business in this*

company. For leaders who do not see how critical quality is to our future—like leaders who could not become boundaryless during the 1980s—GE is simply not the place to be."[404]

~

The Six Sigma quality improvement effort is led by GE employees who've been trained and designated "champions, master black belts, black belts, and green belts."

> *"By January 1998, there will be no one on any slate for consideration for any management job in GE, no matter how junior, without some green belt training. . . ."*[405]

~

When asked how suppliers were responding to demands for higher quality, Welch leapt to his feet and ran to his office and back with the latest studies:

> *"The improvements are already picking up. Many suppliers want to adopt it and spread it across their businesses. Others come as reluctant brides. They do it or they don't supply for us. Suppliers are coming and taking the [Crotonville] course. What we do is, we charge suppliers. What they used to do—when it was free—they'd send along a cluck. Now that we charge them, the quality [of the supplier representative] gets much better; we don't get rich off of it. We just charge them a little."*[406]

~

By the 1997 shareholders meeting, Welch was talking up Six Sigma successes:

> *"We had a billing system at GE Lighting that worked just fine from our perspective. The problem was it didn't mesh very well electronically with the purchasing system at Wal-Mart—one of our best customers. Our system didn't work for them and was causing disputes, delayed payments, and was wasting Wal-Mart's time. A black belt team using Six Sigma methodology, information technology, and $30,000 in investment tackled the problem from Wal-Mart's perspective, and in four months reduced defects in the system by 98 percent. The result for Wal-Mart was higher productivity and competitiveness and fewer disputes and delays—real dollar savings. The result for GE was a return many times that of our investment."*[407]

∽

> *"Just as workout got us to a culture of learning and openness that defined the way we behave, quality improvement, under the disciplined rubric of Six Sigma methodology, will define the way we work."*[408]

∽

Welch explains that superior quality in products and performance is essential because societies the world over have become "value oriented":

"In this environment, a company must be a lean, low-cost producer of quality goods and services in order to survive, let alone prosper."[409]

~

While technology is still critical, Welch says the market is shifting away from the technology leader to the manufacturer that offers basic, good-quality products at the lowest cost. The kind of changes that took place in the medical diagnostic imaging business in the early 1980s are now occurring in many industries:

"In the '60s, medical systems was primarily an X ray business. Product life cycles were measured in years and significant share changes rarely took place. In the mid-'70s, computerized tomography came along, and an industry that hadn't changed in decades was revolutionized in 36 to 48 months. A big, new market was created with brand-new competitors. Share changes were dramatic, and we managed to be winners.

"Today, however [in 1984] medical systems is facing two significant challenges. One is competitive, the need to win in another large new technology— magnetic resonance. The shape of the industry will be redefined over the next year. The second challenge is market change. Medical's customers—hospitals—are under severe pressure to contain costs. Their capital budgets have been cut. Medical, fresh off its CT success, cannot rest."[410]

~

"[W]e must be the best at what we do."[411]

"You're either the best at what you do or you don't do it for very long."[412]

~

Critics say that GE has been slow in embracing the quality movement, and Joseph A. DeFeo of the Juran Institute agrees: "GE in the last decade has done a superb job of driving out cost in their systems. And they got good at that. Through that entire process, to my knowledge, I never met anyone who mentioned the word customer in the context of GE. Rarely was the word customer mentioned. The criticism of GE was that they were becoming very successful in spite of not having quality. They were becoming successful on the cost side. You can only go so far with that."

But, DeFeo added: "I'll tell you this, based on Juran himself (Dr. Joseph Juran was a pioneer in the quality movement), all companies will strive for quality when they have proof of the need. If that were true, then some proof of the need is driving GE. I don't think it's Jack Welch's ego. It would have to be that profitability is suspect, or they're losing market share in certain areas."[413]

The cost of low-quality manufacturing and services, DeFeo explained, can be as high as 20 to 30 percent of a company's revenues.

IT ALL COMES OUT IN THE WASH

An uneasiness all too familiar to working Americans spread through Appliance Park, GE's 40-year-old, 1,500-acre appliance manufacturing facility in the fall of 1992. The Louisville, Kentucky, plant was losing $45 million a year, and the company was about to outsource the domestically built laundry line overseas to save costs. Workers knew that if the troubled washer and dryer business went, it was only a matter of time before refrigerators, ranges, and microwaves went, too. And if that happened, 9,000 jobs could go.

But GE's own principles were at stake as well. What about number 1 or number 2? The appliance business was number 2 domestically, and there had been no serious push to sell internationally.

And what about workout? If GE and its employees couldn't solve problems at Appliance Park, what good were the three Ss—simplicity, speed, and self-confidence—the boundaryless company and all that talk about stretch goals? Welch's management catchwords could be reduced to "ideas du jour."

If GE gave up on large appliances without a serious effort to make them profitable, perhaps the critics were right, that GE is simply a venture capital operation with no commitment to people or products.

GE already had shocked the business world by swapping its small appliance business for a European medical imaging company. Aircaft engines, plastics, and high finance aside, GE's own research shows that 78 percent of the U.S. consumer image of the company is based on appliances.

By closing Appliance Park, GE could face tangible losses as well. Appliances account for 10 percent of GE's annual sales volume. True, the appliance business is tough. But could GE find a place to put its capital to work where it had such a solid foothold and knew the risks?

GE workers knew Appliance Park was in trouble, and GE officials realized the only solution was to completely redesign the old GE washing machine. A financially losing proposition, the machine hadn't been redesigned in a decade. In fact, GE had been using the manufacturing platform for 35 years. A design team was given 20 days to come up with an all new washer.

Knowing full well that Welch was not predisposed to saving the washer line, the team toiled from fall through Christmas. In the meantime, leaders of the International Union of Electronic, Electrical, Salaried, Machine, and Furniture Workers (IUE) negotiated concessions with GE officials. All GE's Louisville employees met at an old park warehouse, working on ideas for greater efficiency. Even Kentucky's governor and lieutenant governor got behind the "Save the Park" effort.

Less than four months after workers were presented with the problem, members of IUE Local 761 approved a new washer design and agreed to a 43-point program to make production more cost-effective. The new washer was the epitome of "lean engineering," using 380 parts instead of 800. The washer was 60 pounds lighter and—with its controversial plastic basket—virtually rust-free.

Appliance Park at Louisville became one of GE's star performing divisions. In 1996, operating margins rose to 11.8 percent of its $6.4 billion in sales, compared to an industry average of 5.7 percent.

In GE's 1996 annual report, David M. Cote, head of GE's appliance business, told just how far the effort had gone. Cote said, "We...strengthened our export product offering with a new international line of home laundry equipment produced at Appliance Park in Louisville, Kentucky. This was the last phase of a $100 million laundry investment that has resulted in significantly higher U.S. market share."[414]

GE's victory in the highly competitive world of home appliances wasn't a sweep. GE failed to edge Whirlpool washers out of Sears stores; and recently, Whirlpool accused GE in Canada of stealing the design of its agitator, the center column that keeps the water and clothes moving during the wash cycle. But GE machines are selling well, and the washer wars are likely to continue.

TAKING STOCK

FAIL YOUR WAY TO SUCCESS

"I failed my way to success," said Thomas Alva Edison, inventor of the lightbulb, and GE's most famous forbear. Jack Welch has survived a few failures himself, some trivial and some that traumatized the company. But, says Welch, like Edison, he has learned. Early on, he blew up a small plant:

> *"It was a pilot plant, probably the size of this [conference] room. I was running a reaction in it and it just—boom—got away and blew up. Our boss at the time was Charlie Reed, who is now 85 years old. This guy, he was the most gentle, thoughtful, caring person. So he asked me to come down and explain what happened, you know. I went down and explained it to him. He's a Ph.D. chemical engineer from MIT, and Charlie Reed and I had this most wonderful conversation about what happened and how it happened. He was like a father to me."[415]*

In 1978, when Welch was sector head of the appliance group, he approved an idea for a revolutionary waterless washing machine that used harmonic vibrations. Four years and nearly $20 million dollars later, GE had a washer the size of a titan missile booster (perhaps a slight exaggeration) that did everything except wash clothes. The concept finally was scrapped. "I was new to the business, the case was persuasive and well-documented, and I supported it," Welch says sheepishly. "It's not the only failure I've had."[416]

~

Regarding GE's dismal attempt to take the lead in factory automation:

> *"We picked the right market but we couldn't have executed [the strategy] much worse. I endorsed everything [the team] did wrong. Somehow or other, they got ahead of themselves in their execution. Until we automated our own dishwasher manufacturing, we really never knew what it was ourselves. We stumbled and fell and tried this and tried that, and then it finally worked. The automation business was folded into a joint venture with Fanuc of Japan and is doing extremely well, and programmable controls have turned out to be a real winner. It won't be a multibillion-dollar business in 1990 [as predicted], but it will be a billion-dollar one making $80 million to $120 million."[417]*

~

About five years into his tenure at GE, it became clear that Welch had failed to fully communicate his philosophy to many employees. An unidentified GE middle manager said: "Jack says, 'Take a swing; if you miss you're okay. But when you sandwich that message together with the other signals in the system, it plays: 'Take a swing, miss, and you're gone.' People still feel the risks are not equal to the rewards."[418]

Welch eventually recognized that he had to do better:

"I was intellectualizing the issues with a couple of hundred people at the top of the company, but clearly I wasn't reaching hundreds of thousands of other people."[419]

～

In 1984, Welch acknowledged the problem in the company publication *Monogram*:

"I recognize that saying these things doesn't make them happen. And I know that if I were out there, it would be terribly frustrating reading this, but not feeling it in my business, in my everyday life. That's why the challenge to create this atmosphere is in all our hands. No one is exempt from either creating it or demanding that it be created."[420]

Welch says that he expanded the scope of his communication, and finally reached many employees by simplifying the message and doggedly repeating it at every opportunity.

~

One event helped Welch progress from his reputation as "Neutron Jack" to "Krypton Jack," after the material that made Superman impenetrable. In 1979, GE positioned its Erie, Pennsylvania, locomotive manufacturing business for a much talked-about revival of American train traffic. After a $300 million investment by GE, the resurrection didn't occur. However, Carl Schlemmer, who headed the locomotive division, gained fame for making a midstream correction. In 1987, Schlemmer cut $65 million from his budget, reversing out of a massive potential loss to make a $34 million profit. In time, the world locomotive market revived and GE became the dominant manufacturer.

> *"The locomotives business is no different from things we've done in plastics and that we've done in other businesses. What we did there is time a market change wrong. We had, when we started that program, perhaps a third of the world market in locomotives. We must now have 75 percent. Why? Because we built a modern factory to take on new technology, and we were there at the wrong time. But it came two years later. And then we were there. Plastics—I never built a plastics plant right yet. It takes two years to build; it always comes on-stream as the economy has dipped a bit. I haven't been right yet. We're a big company. We can afford to make the investment. We can afford to be in there. And we can be wrong on market timing."[421]*

~

Was the acquisition of Kidder Peabody a mistake or did the company fail because of fraud? Or was it some of both? GE acquired an 80 percent interest in Kidder Peabody for $600 million in 1986. In 1995, Welch admitted that the deal "simply didn't work out." Wall Street suffered one of its periodic slumps, which had an impact on Kidder. But worse, Kidder was smacked with two smelly scandals.

Within months of GE's acquisition of the company, Kidder found itself at the center of the Ivan Boesky insider-trading scheme. Kidder's former merger chief, Martin A. Siegel (who left Kidder prior to GE's acquisition of it) pleaded guilty to selling confidential information to Boesky, which he in turn used to his advantage in the stock market. Both Siegel and Boesky served jail time.

> *"I never would have bought Kidder knowing Marty Siegel was a cheat."*[422]

Next, Kidder took a $210 million charge against earnings after bond trader Joe Jett allegedly fabricated $350 million in phony profits. Jett made-up bond trades to boost his own performance-based pay. As Welch put it, Jett operated "a phantom trading scheme, by a single employee, directed not against customers but against the firm itself."[423]

Before the episode was over, Welch was forced to fire an old friend and long-time associate Michael A.

174

Carpenter, who Welch had put in charge of Kidder shortly after the acquisition. GE eventually called it quits and swapped Kidder to PaineWebber for a 25 percent equity in that firm. As part of the deal, Kidder's trading operations were liquidated.

> *"The Kidder story, and its $1.2 billion loss, is not a pleasant one; and it is tempting to simply relegate it to the past—but we can't."*[424]

In reporting to shareholders on the failure, Welch said the big problem was that Kidder wasn't a market leader, therefore it could not withstand the combined pressures of the frauds and of weak trading markets:

> *"This human toll reminds us, once again, that nothing we do is more important than staying competitive—keeping that winning edge. Nothing."*[425]

~

Though Welch talks calmly about the Kidder Peabody fiasco now, he was not calm at the time. Dennis D. Dammerman, senior vice president for finance recalled Welch's reaction: "He yelled, and I yelled, and people yelled back. Were any of us calm for the whole weekend? No, you would've thought we were weird if we had been."[426]

~

Welch expects GE to make other errors as he goes along:

> *"We've made zillions of mistakes, missteps. We made about every mistake there is to be made, I think. See,*

the luxury of being a big company is that you can go to bat often. There's no sense being big if you don't go to bat all the time; then you might as well be small. If you're small, you're faster. So you've got to use your size to keep taking swings. If you bat 75 percent, that's a home run. But if you sit there and act like [you're afraid], then the little companies do everything on you. They kill you. The idea of size is only a strength if you use it. If you go to bat more often, take more swings. I believe that firmly. I think that's a big deal."[427]

~

"I don't mind being wrong. The key is to win a lot more than you lose."[428]

~

GE continues to have trouble spots. The most recent was GE Capital's $1 billion investment in Montgomery Ward & Co. In 1997, the company went into Chapter 11, reorganization bankruptcy. Welch sent in a "Mr. Fix It" from Toys "R" Us to resolve Ward's financial difficulties. GE Capital Services also is doing salvage work. Montgomery Ward will close marginal stores, refinance debt, and develop a new business plan, and GE Capital hopes to sell Ward's Signature direct-mail unit for $1 billion and use the money to pay off debt.[429]

~

In retrospect, Welch sometimes wishes he'd been tougher sooner:

> *"My biggest mistake was agonizing too much over difficult decisions. I should have done it faster. But we're all human. We don't like to face up to some of the unpleasant things; removing somebody is the most unpleasant thing you have to do in life. And I didn't want to break this company. In hindsight, I was generally erring on the side of being afraid of breaking it. GE would be better off if I had acted faster."[430]*

WELCH'S CRITICS

General Electric has been targeted by several activist groups seeking social, environmental, and other reform. For example, in 1991, the Sisters of St. Francis in Philadelphia ordered their college, high school, and 12 hospitals to boycott GE products. Additionally, the sister's pension funds divested all but a token amount of GE stock.

"We consider this a peace and justice issue," said Sister Miriam Eileen Murray. The Sisters of St. Francis joined Infact, a Boston-based activist group, in protesting GE's production of nuclear weapons. Infact also took its anti-GE, antinuclear weapon campaign to the Catholic Health Association, where several other religious orders decided to boycott GE products until the company that claims to "bring good things to life" got out of the death and destruction business.[431]

Infact claimed the boycott cost GE $30 million in medical-equipment contracts—mostly to hospitals and medical services operated by religious organizations.[432] A GE executive said GE never felt any impact from the boycott. GE sold its aerospace business (the unit in question) to Martin Marietta during the aerospace industry consolidation in the early 1990s.

∼

GE also has taken heat for selling Lexan, one of its plastics, to a company called Tecnovar, which used the plastic as a component in land mines. Through a circuitous route, Tecnovar's land mines made their way to Rwanda, where the ruling Hutu government used them in the massacre of 500,000 Tutsi tribesmen. Human Rights Watch is asking companies that manufacture materials for land mines to take steps to make sure the material isn't used for these randomly murderous devices. While 17 companies that supply materials have agreed to take such safeguards, GE has not.[433]

NOTE: GE says it does not—and will not—sell plastics to land mine manufacturers. GE plastics may have made their way into land mines through a third party or downstream distributor, a possibility that GE says is impossible to prevent.

∼

Criticism of Welch's management style may have prompted the "software" or cultural revolution at GE.

Tom Peters, the famed management consultant, worked with GE at one time. Insiders say Welch and Peters became "mutually disillusioned" with one another. Peters once called Welch's style "management by fear."

Peters told *The Wall Street Journal* in 1988 that, under Welch, GE had indeed changed. Once "the most glorious technology company of the century, GE has become a hodgepodge."[434]

Peters wrote in his 1987 book, *In Search of Excellence* "If Mad Jack hasn't bought or sold one or two businesses in a day, it's a crappy day for him. Welch belongs with the J.P. Morgans and other financial wizards."[435] Peters says GE is one of the few clients he has ever quit.

In recent years though, Peters began sounding like a Welch fan. In a 1994 *Forbes* interview he said:

"The chairman is spouting 'liberation,' 'small and beautiful,' and something called 'workout' in the '90s, but the '80s was his decade. He turned his dogs into dog food (selling off the likes of Utah International) and coined (literally as well as figuratively) his Boston Consulting-Group-look-alike approach: All GE businesses would be number 1, or number 2, or number 3 in their industry, or out they'd go. Michael Porter didn't like it. (And I wasn't that keen on it either.) Except it worked. Good advice for the '90s: Milk the cows, harvest the dogs, and worry not whether linguist supreme Bill Safire pillories you for metaphorical mayhem."[436]

$\sim$

Vincent Morelli, who was chief executive of GE-CGR, GE's medical systems business in Europe, partially defends Welch against Peters' charges: "Just because Welch is such an intelligent and fearsome character doesn't mean it's management by fear. But he does scare a lot of people—even good ones."[437]

～

"Loyalty here is 24 hours deep," claimed an unidentified employee in 1987. "Welch has lost the dedication of a couple hundred thousand people. He's done a remarkable job of changing the emphasis of the company. But is the price bigger than the company should be paying?"[438]

～

Even after Welch began promoting a simpler approach to work, Mark Markovitz, an engineer at GE's Schenectady facility, wrote in a 1989 letter to *Fortune*: "Jack Welch berates GE managers and professionals who must work 90 hours a week to get their jobs done. I know many of them. I am one of them. We are spending the time on customer service, engineering, development, manufacturing, cost reduction, quality control, and trouble-shooting problems because many of our colleagues were nuked by Welch. Is this bureaucratic work?

"Jack Welch's predecessors—Ralph Cordiner, Fred Borch, and Reginald Jones—nurtured the aircraft engine, gas turbine, and plastics businesses when they were small or money-losing operations. What chance of survival would they have had under Mr. Welch's number 1 or number 2 test?"[439]

~

Despite reforms later in Welch's term, GE has room for improvement. "GE is too political, because all large organizations are political, but it is less political than most corporations I've been associated with," claims Steve Kerr, director of GE's management training center at Crotonville.

Kerr adds that as Welch becomes more of an icon, and as some of his contemporaries leave GE to head other companies, there is a greater tendency to "agree with the boss. The Jimminy Crickets are gone. I would like to see more people pushing back." Kerr says though Welch is aware when someone is toadying, he often seems to ignore it.[440]

~

Jacques Robinson, a former GE vice president said: "Jack's ideal manager is strong, independent, a great leader, and will agree with him."[441]

~

After GE acquired RCA and its plum subsidiary NBC, Welch tried very hard to keep NBC President Grant Tinker on the staff. Welch's NBC, as it turned out, wasn't Tinker's cup of tea, who said, "I look at Jack as two guys. He's a good guy you can hang out with, a man's man. The same guy walks into an office and he's a chess player. People aren't people anymore."[442]

Tinker, like others, seems to have softened in recent years. After an article appeared in *Fortune* magazine about GE's success with NBC, Tinker wrote to Welch:

"[The story is] a more public version of what I (and many others) have been saying about NBC for a couple of years. They're simply too smart and too fast for the competition. I'd write a book about it, but then nobody read my first one."[443]

~

When Ted Turner's "mouth of the South" blasted Welch, it caused a media flap. *Vanity Fair* magazine reported (and several national newspapers repeated) that media mogul Ted Turner called Welch a "Hitler." Turner supposedly said this to Steve Brill when discussing details of the agreement under which Warner bought Brill's *American Lawyer* magazine and Court TV. Brill wanted to buy back the assets with financial backing from NBC. Turner refused, afraid that NBC would gain control of the magazine and the TV channel. "Welch is a Hitler, and they're building nuclear bombs over there, and I'm not going to let them have it," Turner allegedly spouted. Joyce Hergenhan, GE spokesperson replied: "GE doesn't build nuclear bombs, and we have no comment on what Mr. Turner may or may not have said." Turner earlier had apologized to Jewish community leaders for calling Rupert Murdoch a Hitler.[444]

NOTE: GE does not make nuclear weapons. The company once built nuclear power plants, and still provides services to operating facilities. GE also built nonnuclear components for missiles on which nuclear weapons can be delivered, but that business was sold to Lockheed Martin.

THE GERMAN POINT OF VIEW

In a 1997 article entitled "The Brutal Manager," the German magazine *Der Speigel* gave Welch a grilling. The following translation is just a sample of the three dozen questions *Der Speigel* posed to Welch.

SPEIGEL: You are seen as the man who nuked factory buildings. Does that bother you?

WELCH: That's a bit over the top. We went through a difficult time, that's true. But we had to get through it. We had to sell businesses and make people redundant. That was painful for everyone and the worst part of my job. But we gave the people decent compensation packages. We didn't throw anyone onto the streets just like that.

～

SPEIGEL: As the number of employees was halved, the share price increased almost twentyfold. Were the wallets of the shareholders more important to you than the families of your former employees?

WELCH: No. When we started restructuring General Electric, it was easy for everyone to find a new job. If we had waited, it would have been worse for everyone. In a global economy, you cannot manage a company in a paternalistic way just because it feels better. If you don't sort things out, in good time they will eventually explode in your face. Then you have to become brutal and cruel.

~

SPEIGEL: You can hardly talk of unbridled joy amongst your workforce. You are notorious for your stretch goals, which you use to set your employees almost impossible targets.

WELCH: If you want to instill enthusiasm for an idea in 240,000 people, you can't be soft and gentle. To some extent, you have to be an extremist. Naturally, we sometimes fail to reach our targets. But at least our people try their very best. They put in a tremendous amount of effort and give everything they have to offer. And they know that they will be rewarded; for example, with share options. In our company, people go after their dreams. They don't achieve that if they are set unchallenging budget targets.

~

SPEIGEL: You have the most valuable company in the world, your profit margins are admired by the entire industry, and yet you will not rest. Does growth have no limits for you?

WELCH: No, no, no. As early as the eighties, people used to say to me again and again that I finally had squeezed the lemon dry. Look at where we are today: My people grow with their responsibilities; Jack Welch grows every day; the whole company is growing because we have such a productive atmosphere. There are no limits to productivity; we will never run out of ideas.

~

SPEIGEL: In your company, an average worker would have to work more than a thousand years to earn the same amount of money [as Welch does]. Is that fair?

WELCH: We don't go out into the streets and force people into our factories at gunpoint. Everyone who works for us is here because he wants to earn money and develop himself intellectually. The wages I pay are adequate and the atmosphere here is so exciting that they all want to stay. So where's the problem?[445]

BEING A GOOD CITIZEN

Healthy corporations, says Welch, can be better citizens than weak ones:

"Healthy businesses pay taxes. Healthy businesses create increased employment. Healthy businesses create an ambience that's much more attractive than the insecurities and tensions associated with weak businesses. So I believe it is my responsibility to

bring together, and nurture, growing businesses that are healthy, and to get more businesses into that category while minimizing the businesses that are in trouble."[446]

~

For part of the 1980s, GE paid little or nothing in federal taxes. The company took large write-offs allowed under the provisions for federal investment tax credit. In a 1986 speech, Welch defended GE's tax-free status and protested the end of the investment tax credit by the federal government:

"Since Mr. Reagan's tax plan went into effect in 1981, with its provisions for investment tax credit and accelerated cost recovery, General Electric and its finance subsidiary have invested $18 billion in their own plants and in the factories, utilities, airlines, and railroads of America, creating or preserving at least 250,000 jobs.

"In addition to those jobs, that tax policy allowed GE to modernize and automate its factories to become more competitive in world markets. That competitiveness allowed us to swim upstream against the import flood and achieve a $2.6 billion trade surplus last year alone.

"Tax incentives to invest ... and compete ... and win ... work. They worked for my company and for America."[447]

~

"I have heard it said that federal tax policy should not be used to affect industrial policy. My question is, why not? We allow deductions to encourage charitable contributions, furthering social objectives. Churches are aided by tax laws, as is housing . . . and a hundred other worthy causes."[448]

NOTE: When investment tax credits were eliminated, GE began paying federal taxes again. GE paid $3.5 billion in U.S. federal income taxes in 1996. No figure was available on how much GE paid to state and local governments or the governments of other countries in which it operated.

~

Welch says that business and government are partners in creating a functional, prosperous society:

"The prime minister of Malaysia meets with business leaders all the time. Mahathir Mohamad is his name. He said to me, 'Look, I own 40 percent of you. You are my employees. Your success is critical to my programs. If I am going to build roads and build education, I need you to be successful because I get 40 percent of your revenues in taxes. I'm your biggest shareowner.' That philosophy is so powerful. He said, 'with your success I can educate Malays, I can build roads. I can implement the vision of 20/20,' which is his vision of what Malaysia will be—every person educated. He sends thousands [of students] out to the rest of the world to go to college.

They have to come back within five years, [to get the] free college. This guy has got it down. He understands, business isn't the enemy, business is the partner. *The successful business makes Malaysia win, because he's the largest shareowner. I always thought that philosophy was the clearest articulation of the role of government in business that I ever saw. Our largest shareowner by far is the U.S. government. They get billions in tax revenue from us and that's their dividend. They get more dividends than we pay out to all of our shareowners combined. I'm not criticizing anyone with that. I'm saying how positive that is. When you look at the success of Malaysia. Malaysia is looking more like Singapore every day—fantastic growth in GDP, no inflation. So the model is working."*[449]

∽

General Electric has been vilified for damaging the environment, an accusation that Welch insists is unfair. Nevertheless, since 1985, the River Cafe and the Water Club restaurants in New York have posted signs saying GE's top executives are not welcome there, due to "General Electric's flagrant, pernicious, and continuing pollution of the Hudson River spawning grounds of the striped bass." A GE plant in Hudson Falls, New York, once routinely and legally discharged toxic PCBs (polychlorinated biphenyls) into the Hudson River. The practice ended in 1977 when it became known that PCBs were harmful to fish and other living organisms. The PCBs, however, are still in the river and some environmentalists want them dredged out. While recent environmental efforts have brought a large number of fish back to the Hudson, the striped bass are still inedible.[450]

~

But, claims Welch, GE is innocent:

> *"There's no question that nobody who polluted in the '50s and '60s knew a thing about the fact that they were polluting. I was a Ph.D. chemical engineer from a great school. I came to Pittsfield, Massachusetts and* bathed *in Phenol in those days. We never had one course from '57 to '60 dealing with the environment. It wasn't part of the chemicals we did. We worked in it, we bathed in it. We did things. I can see trucks driving out of my plant now with waste chemicals that I sold to a waste company. I don't know where the hell they went. Now we say how bad they were, those polluters. It was not mean."[451]*

~

But a lesson was learned from the mistakes of the 1950s and 1960s, Welch says:

> *"[W]hen you go into a country, and the [environmental] laws aren't there, you've just got to know that the laws are going to be there. Because it's the right thing to do. Today, our awareness must be translated globally. We can't go into Mexico unless*

we put in good water systems, treatment centers, all those things. Even though their laws aren't there, 20 years from now the laws will be there. And it's the right thing to do."[452]

~

Long before politicians took it up as a rallying cry, GE workers were encouraged to volunteer to make their communities better places to live. In 1990, GE was given Harvard's George S. Dively Award for Leadership in Corporate Public Initiative.

Welch often praises GE volunteers, especially those who help raise education standards in the communities in which they live and work:

> *"American business did not cause what's happening in our inner cities and rural schools—this waste of so many young minds. World economic forces, technology, and demographic factors are at its root; but we will be accessories if we do nothing to change things. None of us can escape the social costs and pressures this waste is generating."*[453]

~

Welch received a letter describing a high school graduation ceremony in Burkville, Alabama, one of the poorest rural areas in the country, and home to a GE plastics plant. Many graduating seniors received GE scholarships:

> *"The woman who wrote the letter described the scene as dozens of GE scholars, poor kids who never*

would have had a chance to attend college, marched up the aisle to receive their scholarships. The cheers, tears, joy, and hope she described made for as moving a scene as you could imagine."[454]

~

In the mid-1980s, Elfun, GE's management society, decided to help American youth become better educated:

"One of the first high schools they tackled was in Cincinnati, Ohio, the home of our aircraft engines business. This particular school was sending three students a year to college out of a graduating class of 305—1 percent—but it had a zealot named Jack Schroder as principal, who is committed to improving things. With his support, over a hundred of our people—long-time employees, new hires, retirees—linked up with students who wanted help, and acted as mentors, advisors, helping with problems, academic or otherwise. They were always a phone call away—and they cared. They were a window into a world these kids had never really experienced—a world of work, study, achievement, and success. They didn't bat 1000, but one statistic tells the story. The school that in 1985 sent three to college sent 73 this year—from one in 100 to 1 in 4—and they are committed to 1 in 2 by 1994."[455]

One of the students who benefited was a Cincinnati girl whose parents opposed her going to college.

"Encouraged by her GE mentor, she is now in the fourth year of a five-year architecture program at the University of Kentucky."[456]

~

In explaining GE's commitment to volunteerism, especially in education, Welch said:

"The global battles in virtually every manufacturing industry are now being won or lost on productivity, on speed, on responsiveness to change. The low-skilled, well-paid work of the postwar era has been designed out, automated, or is done in low-wage areas overseas. Companies can no longer hire people who cannot quickly add the type of value required by an ever more demanding and competitive marketplace.

"This upward racheting of required entry skills, in combination with the awful pathologies of our inner city and rural school systems, have moved the bottom rung of that American ladder so far beyond the grasp of many of our young people that they no longer even bother to reach. This is at a time when American industries, beset by brutal competition and buffeted by change, need fresh, eager, creative young minds that are excited by change rather than frightened or paralyzed by it. How applicable the motto of the United Negro College Fund: A mind truly is a terrible thing to waste. We are wasting them by the millions."[457]

~

Welch loves volunteerism but dislikes government bureaucracy:

"People say that now that the Soviet Union is out of business we have no more truly dangerous enemies. They're wrong. The Soviets couldn't beat us, but economically, the bureaucracy and bureaucrats still can."[458]

～

On the other hand:

"It's not enough to complain about bloat and fat in the federal budget when we have it in our own budgets; or to complain about government bureaucracy when we're up to our ears in staff. Or to demand incentives to invest and then fail to invest aggressively. Or to approach Washington as a pack of clamoring special-interest groups with little thought for a coherent policy that's best for all."[459]

～

What are Welch's personal politics? Though he often praised Presidents Reagan and Bush while they were in office, he seldom mentions President Clinton publicly, though he has visited the Clinton White House. Welch describes his personal politics this way:

"I'm to the right of center fiscally and to the left of center socially. I used to be left of center fiscally. When I first got this job, I thought—with the exception of Reg Jones—there were a bunch of raving

right-wingers running this company. As you stay with the company a long time and deal with government, fiscally you move to the right. I hope I don't sound as bad as they did, but I sound more like them 17 years later than I did when I started."

By "left of center" on social issues, Welch means:

"[I]'m a big supporter of soft landings for employees. I do believe strongly that we've got to give people more equal opportunity. We've got to do everything we can to break down the barriers. I meet twice a year with the African-American forum. The women's issue has taken care of itself—we used to have all these dinners and we had one recently. But, generally speaking, it's an African-American issue in terms of movement, supply, opportunity.

"We just concluded our sixth labor contract [under Welch's watch and 10 overall] without a blip. We do that because we believe in fair treatment. We kept management rights that we want, and yet we're a wealthy company enough to pay and if they're wounded [by lay offs], if anyone has got 30 years service and impacted, they get benefits. We like our labor force. We don't have these contentious relations. We're all partners in the same game."[460]

HOW MUCH IS LEADERSHIP WORTH?

At GE's 1997 annual meeting, Teamsters union pension fund managers proposed that in the future, Jack

Welch's salary be capped at $1 million per year unless put to a shareholders' vote. In 1996, Welch received $6.3 million in salary, $15.1 million from a long-term incentive program, and $6.2 million by exercising options on GE stock for a total pay package of $28.2 million. Additionally, Welch was paid almost $600,000 in benefits such as life insurance. His wage, complained the unions, was 148 times that paid to the average GE worker.

Business Week estimated that Welch also held another $107 million in unexercised stock options. "The issue is the competitive marketplace," Welch told shareholders. "The market is willing to pay at a certain level." The proposal restricting Welch's pay failed with only 9 percent of shareholders voting in favor of it.[461]

~

A year earlier Welch, the 15th highest-paid CEO in the United States, explained his situation to a Japanese business magazine:

> *"We CEOs also live in a market economy. A company can trade a capable CEO for $20 million, just like with a professional baseball player. A new word called a CEO market has arrived in the United States"*[462]

~

Andrew Bary, "The Trader" columnist for *Barron's* says that Welch has earned his pay:

"Welch has come under fire for his compensation, which last year totaled $21 million, but under his leadership, GE has created more wealth for shareholders than any other company in America."[463]

Allan Sloan, *Newsweek* business columnist, sees it differently. In writing about executive salaries, Welch's included, Sloan said: "To Wall Street, these guys are gods who can't be overpaid. To Main Street, though, this isn't pay for performance; it's just plain piggery."[464]

∽

To continue its battle against excessive executive pay packages, the AFL-CIO launched a World Wide Web site (www.ctsg.com/ceopay) to inform both workers and investors.

PASSING
THE TORCH

WHO WILL PULL THE SWORD
FROM THE STONE?

Two years after having triple-bypass heart surgery
Welch says:

> *"[T]he doctors tell me I've never been better. I exer-
> cise every morning, I do three miles on a very steep
> treadmill at a good pace. I play 36 holes of golf, and
> I play comfortably. I walk the whole way. I'd say I
> have more energy than I had 10 years ago."*[465]

Welch travels extensively and maintains a demanding
work schedule. Nevertheless, at the end of the year
2000, he will retire from GE. Welch often deftly
deflects questions about his succession plans. When
asked what he is thinking about for the future: "I'm
thinking about Six Sigma," he flashes back, in refer-
ence to GE's all-encompassing quality improvement
program.

A GE executive close to Welch supported the
silence surrounding the CEO's retirement plans. "I

don't know why everyone is making such a fuss. This event is three and a half years away."[466]

When Welch was hospitalized with heart trouble, succession at GE became a big fuss. Welch first underwent angioplasty, and while recuperating, he sent a memo to two dozen top executives. According to *Fortune*: "He pointed out that the day after news of his heart problem hit Wall Street, GE stock climbed nearly a dollar. While the run-up was convincing evidence of investors' confidence in GE's management team, Welch told officers he had no intention of pulling a stunt like that again just to prove them right."[467]

Ten days later Welch underwent quintuple-bypass surgery, and the stock held steady, but newspapers screamed that a crisis was at hand, since there was no apparent successor to Welch. That is far from the truth. In an interview with the French magazine *L'Expansion*, Welch painted the real picture: "It's like an obsession. I'm always talking about it with Paolo Fresco [the vice chairman], even when we go out for a drink. What's so-and-so like; can he take a balanced view of things; or to what extent does he bring in new ideas? It's on my mind constantly, and finding the right person is the most important thing I can do for my group at the moment."[468]

Fortune magazine reported that there is a confidential list of two to three candidates within GE capable of taking over. Additionally, each May and November, directors review the files of 15 or so top managers. They maintain dossiers based on long interviews with bosses, associates, and subordinates. "Directors probe the managers' strengths and weaknesses, contribute suggestions for their development, and debate future assignments," Welch says. "Should the day come to open the envelope, the board will be prepared to make a considered decision, rather than rubber-stamp an insider's recommendation."[469]

Despite Welch's strong health and high energy, Steve Kerr says he believes Welch intends to step down as planned: "When an idea comes along that he doesn't like, he says, 'that goes on the 2001 list,'" apparently to be reconsidered when Welch is out of office.[470]

Welch may prefer to stay mum on the subject of his retirement to prevent turmoil in the company. When he was chosen as the new chief executive officer, top executives were subjected to a grueling four-year competition that demoralized workers and kept GE focused on internal problems rather than serving customers, competing for new business, and developing new products. Welch agreed that it was brutal.

Welch says he intends to choose a successor less stressfully:

"I hope so. But you know, the process ended up, for better or worse, okay. We lost talent, but I think you'd lose talent if you did it nicely. Because these people are just too strong. I'm going to try to do it differently, I'm not going to have it quite as glaringly a race. And so far—knock on wood—we don't see any signs of it affecting teamwork. Things got to a point the last time of becoming very political. With

each other. Not with Reg [Reginald Jones, Welch's predecessor]. Reg handled it beautifully. The people were all just siding with each other; camps were being formed in the company. Pray to God that doesn't happen."[471]

Welch has made it clear to the contenders that if there is any throat-cutting, it will be the person's own throat that gets cut, say insiders. Yet, the tongue-wagging and speculation have begun. In the summer of 1997, a half-dozen top GE officials were shuffled from one job to another, apparently to give them more experience and allow them to be evaluated in new ways. A *Forbes* article eliminated any GE executive over the age of 51 as candidates, since GE likes executives to have a long run at the job. Typically, a CEO spends 12 to 15 years in the corner office, with a view of the woods surrounding GE headquarters.

"A GE chief executive doesn't have to serve 15 to 20 years, but I think you need to serve 10 years, otherwise you get these insane moves. I've seen some companies like that. During my time as CEO, there have been five CEOs in some places; six in some places. You show up at meetings and there's another one there. When the people are only there a couple of years, everybody's trying to do something, make their stamp quickly. And so I think you should live with your errors. Work on them. Business is a series of processes; they're not perfect."[472]

Considering the amount of time and money GE spends grooming executives, probably a candidate will be chosen from inside the company. And even when the older executives are struck from the list, there is no shortage of candidates at GE. The front list includes: David Calhoun, 40, CEO of GE Lighting; David Cote, 44, CEO of Appliances; Jeffrey Immelt, 41, CEO of Medical Systems; James McNernety, 47, CEO of GE Aircraft Engine; Robert Nardelli, 49, CEO of Power Systems; Gary Reiner, 42, senior vice president, chief information officer, GE; and James Rogers, 48, CEO, Industrial Control.

David Cote (pronounced coat-ee) is seen as the front-runner by many. He's young, and he has been spotlighted in *The Wall Street Journal* and *Fortune* for his quick-witted leadership and globalization of the appliance division.

Technically, Welch will not choose his own successor. But the board of directors most likely will accept Welch's recommendation. An anonymous insider says: "I think Jack will pick someone like himself: young, self-confident, with two brains and boundless energy."[473]

In the end, Welch's legacy will be the business. He hopes to leave behind "a company that's able to change at least as fast as the world is changing, and people whose real income is secure because they're winning and whose psychic income is rising because every person is participating."[474]

∿

"My successor, hopefully, will shed some cards and do things differently. That's what the process is all about—bringing in fresh ideas—but it's not any implication of what the predecessor did, at least in my case. My predecessor did a terrific job."[475]

~

"The day I go home, I'll disappear from the place and the person who comes in will do it their way."[476]

~

What will Jack Welch do with his time, energy, and intellect once he retires? Virtually any corporation in the world would welcome him on the board, or even as CEO. And he could always teach. "He's an ideal student, if you are a teacher; and he is the ideal teacher, if you are a dean. He's as good as any faculty member I have," says Kerr.[477]

Indeed, when Welch leaves GE, he will not be shoved out the door with a gold watch. Welch will continue to work up to 30 days a year as a part-time "ambassador" for GE, paid at the rate of his daily salary at the time of his retirement. And he'll have use of GE facilities and equipment—ranging from the copier to the corporate jet—free of charge. A company spokesperson says that in light of Welch's role in creating more than $150 billion in shareholder value, it is in the company's best interest that Welch remain available for consultation.[478]

~

Despite Welch's charismatic leadership, Kerr says: "The company will do well after Welch because the company has always done well."[479]

SUMMING UP

Perhaps this message from Jack Welch to President-elect Bill Clinton in 1992 would summarize what Welch learned at GE:

> *"Since everyone else will be handing out gratuitous advice to President-elect Clinton, I guess I can too: Americans are winners by nature, not whiners. Don't baby or patronize them or try to protect them. Appeal to their competitiveness, challenge them to break the barriers that separate and slow them down. Keep the bureaucrats and industrial policy types away from their enterprises; let them go and watch what happens. No one who has done that has ever been disappointed."[480]*

～

After he became chairman of GE, Welch continued to grow and evolve, which many people say is his greatest strength. Writes Noel Tichy: "Having started out as the man with the bullhorn, in effect yelling at subordinates who couldn't keep pace, he evolved into a coach, willing to pause (for a nanosecond or two) to help others along."[481]

～

What does Welch think of himself and his life at GE?:

"I've been in a series of lucky places. It takes a lot of experiences, a lot of luck. Luck is at least 60 percent."[482]

~

Welch sees himself as part of a continuing story:

"I didn't fix GE. I'm often described as 'fixing' GE. All I did was take GE and get it ready for the next period of time. But GE didn't need a lot of fixing. It was well done by my predecessor."[483]

~

What would Welch tell a young person who aspires to becoming chief executive officer at a company like General Electric?

"I would never tell anyone how to become CEO of GE because I don't know how it happens. But I would say the things I talk about when I teach [the Crotonville leadership] course. All about energy, energize, and edge—E cubed, I call it. You've got to have incredible energy to lead any organization. You've got to be on fire, if you will. It's a part of it. You've got to be able to energize people. You've got to care about them; they have to believe you care about them. You can have all the energy in the world, but if you don't get other people energized, nothing happens. The ability to energize, excite, bring in, share; it is the most exciting thing."[484]

Welch takes pride in how GE, through such devices as the employee stock option plan, can help people make their dreams come true:

"Think about it! Their kids can go to school; they can build a second home—every dream. So we've changed the game of this bureaucracy so that more people are participating."[485]

~

There is no question that Welch will leave his mark on the business world when he retires from GE. Paolo Fresco, the second in command at GE, says Welch already is the most imitated business leader anywhere: "If Jack decided to start walking on his head one morning, everyone would do likewise."[486]

~ ✳ ~

GENERAL ELECTRIC AND JACK WELCH

• CHRONOLOGY •

1878: Edison Electric Light Co. was founded with $300,000 to commercialize Thomas A. Edison's breakthroughs in electricity, the incandescent lamp. The first practical application of the technology was the lighting of the steamship Columbia in 1880. Soon afterward, Edison Electric built an individual lighting system for the Holborn Viaduct in London and the Pearl Street Station in New York City.

1889: Edison Electric merged with Thomson-Houston Electric Co. to form the General Electric Co. Edison was disappointed that the company did not retain his name and attended only one board meeting. He continued to serve as a consultant and to collect royalties on his inventions.

1895: GE began to manufacture the most powerful locomotive in the world.

1896: The Dow Jones Industrial Index was created. General Electric was among the 30 companies included.

1899: GE paid its first quarterly dividend. Dividends have been paid each quarter since.

1905: GE made the first toaster.

1915: GE produced the first electric refrigerator.

1932: The consumer credit division was formed to finance refrigerators. The first washing machine was rolled out.

1935: John Francis Welch Jr. was born November 19, in Peabody, Massachusetts, to John Francis and Grace Welch.

1942: GE manufactured its first aircraft engine; and to supply Allied forces in World War II, factories worked to capacity.

1954: GE designed the first jet engine that propelled an airplane at twice the speed of sound.

1956: The GE Management Development Institute at Crotonville, New York, was established.

1957: Jack Welch graduated from University of Massachusetts with honors, BS in chemical engineering.

1959: Welch married Carolyn B. Osburn, November 1959. Several senior GE executives were found guilty of a price-fixing scheme with Westinghouse. The executives were fired, but the incident raised questions about CEO Ralph Cordiner's aggressive "management by objectives" program.

1960: Welch earned a doctorate in chemical engineering at the University of Illinois. Welch joined General Electric's plastics division in Pittsfield, Massachusetts. He was responsible for the technical development of Noryl, a plastic resin.

1961: Following a lukewarm raise at GE Plastics, Welch accepted a position as a chemical engineer in Chicago. Before he started the new job, GE induced Welch back with a raise and a promotion.

1963: Welch was placed in charge of the chemical development operation.

1968: At age 33, Welch became GE's youngest general manager ever. He was given charge of the plastics business department, which included new products like Lexan and Noryl.

1972: Welch was promoted to vice president.

1973: At age 37, Welch became group executive for the $1.5 billion components and materials group, which included all of plastics, plus GE Medical Systems.

1977: Welch was named senior vice president and sector executive for the consumer products and services sector. At the same time, he became vice chairman of GE Credit Corporation.

1978: GE built the world's largest nuclear power plant, Tokai-Mura in Japan.

1979: Welch was named vice chairman and executive officer. Three Mile Island nuclear power plant accident destroyed already shaky consumer confidence in nuclear energy. Orders evaporated for GE-built nuclear reactors.

1980: GE opened a new dishwasher plant in Louisville, Kentucky, in the first phase of $1 billion investment in major appliances.

1981: On April 1, John F. Welch, 45, became the 8th chairman of GE. GE's shares, adjusted for splits, were trading at around $4 and the company's market value was $12 billion, 11th in the stock market. Earnings were $1.65 billion on sales of $27.24 billion.

1982: Welch's phase 1, or "hardware" restructuring began. GE invested $300 million in automating its locomotive business and another $130 million to expand the R&D center in Schenectady, New York. The air-conditioning business was sold. The television show *60 Minutes* criticized GE for closing a clothes iron plant in Ontario, California, that seemed to be making money.

1983: GE sold its housewares division to Black & Decker for about $300 million.

1984: *Fortune* magazine called Welch the "Toughest Boss in America." GE sold Utah International mining operations to BHP of Australia for $2.4 billion, and acquired Employers Reinsurance Corporation for $1.1 billion.

1985: In December, GE announced it would buy the Radio Corporation of America for $6.3 billion in cash. NBC Television was an RCA Subsidiary. GE sold its interest in Australian coal fields for $390 million. The hardware phase of the Welch revolution was completed. As a precursor to phase 2, Welch began "delayering" and then reshuffling top management. GE was indicted and pleaded guilty to improper time-card charges on a defense contract. Welch and his wife Carolyn divorced after 28 years of marriage, a reportedly amicable separation.

1987: GE acquired a Miami television station for $270 million, D&K Financial for $100 million, swapped its consumer electronics business for the medical equipment business of Thomson S.A., and acquired Gelco Corp. for $250 million. GE sold North America Co. for Life & Health for $200 million.

1988: Welch began the "software" revolution at GE in earnest. The concept of "workout" was born. The semiconductor business was sold to Harris Corporation. GE also sold RCA Global Communications for $160 million and five radio stations for $122 million. GE acquired Montgomery Ward's credit card operation for $1 billion, Roper Corp. for $510 million and Borg-Warner's plastics business for $2.3 billion.

1989: In April, Welch married investment lawyer Jane Beasley. GE launched its innovative workout program.

1991: GE passed IBM as the nation's most valued corporation.

1993: Joe Jett's phantom trading scheme bilked Kidder Peabody for $210 million in net income.

1994: Kidder Peabody's trading operation was liquidated and the investment firm was swapped for 25 percent equity in PaineWebber.

1995: Welch underwent quintuple-bypass heart surgery. GE launched its Six Sigma quality control effort.

1996: GE achieved $150 billion market capitalization, largest of any company in the world. It was the most profitable company in the United States.

1997: GE was the first company in the world to achieve a $200 billion market capitalization. Welch was inducted into the National Business Hall of Fame in Cincinnati.

2000: Jack Welch expected to retire at age 65.

ENDNOTES

1. Tim Smart, "Jack Welch's Encore," *Business Week*, October 28, 1996, p. 154.

2. Charles R. Day, Jr. and Polly LaBarre, "GE: Just Your Average Everday $60 Billion Family Grocery Store," *Industry Week*, May 2, 1994

3. Marilyn Harris, Zachary Schiller, Russell Mitchell, and Christopher Power, "Can Jack Welch Reinvent GE?" *Business Week*, June 30, 1986, p. 62.

4. R. Corelli and V. Dwyer, "Jack Welch Reinvents GE—Again," *The Economist*, March 30, 1991, p. 59.

5. Laura Landro, "GE's Wizards Turning from the Bottom Line to Share of the Market," *The Wall Street Journal*, July 12, 1982.

6. Janet Guyon, "GE Chairman Welch, Though Much Praised, Starts to Draw Critics," *The Wall Street Journal*, August 4, 1988.

7. Tim Smart, "Jack Welch's Encore," *Business Week*, October 28, 1996, p. 154.

8. Ralph Nader and William Taylor, *The Big Boys: Power and Position in American Business*, (New York: Pantheon Books, 1986), p. xv.

9. Mark Potts, "GE's Management Mission," *The Washington Post*, May 22, 1988.

10. David Warshaw, "Sharing at Every Level," *Monogram*, January-February, 1987.

11. Christopher Lorenz, "Life Under Jack Welch: Opportunistic and Tough," *Financial Times*, May 15, 1998.

12. Russell Mitchell and Judith H. Dobrzynski, "GE's Jack Welch: How Good a Manager Is He?" *Business Week*, December 14, 1987.

13. Frank Swoboda, "Jack Welch and the Boundaryless Company," *The Washington Post*, February 27, 1994.

14. Eric Gelman and Penelope Wang, *Newsweek*, December 23, 1985.

15. J.P. Donlon, "Chief Executive of the Year," *Chief Executive*, July/August, 1993.

16. Noel Tichy and Stratford Sherman, *Control Your Own Destiny or Someone Else Will* (New York: Currency Doubleday, 1993), p. 126.

17. Jack Egan, "What Makes GE Keep Growing," *U.S. News and World Report*, November 23, 1987.

18. Ken Auletta, *Three Blind Mice: How the TV Networks Lost Their Way* (New York: Random House, 1991), p. 17.

19. Ibid., p. 240.

20. Ibid., p. 545.

21. Janet Guyon, "GE Chairman Welch, Though Much Praised, Starts to Draw Critics," *The Wall Street Journal*, August 4, 1988.

22. Auletta, *Three Blind Mice: How the TV Networks Lost Their Way*, p. 326.

23. Ibid.

24. Guyon, "GE Chairman Welch, Though Much Praised, Starts to Draw Critics."

25. Auletta, *Three Blind Mice: How the TV Networks Lost Their Way*, p. 393.

26. Ibid., p. 327.

27. Ibid., p. 222.

28. Ibid., p. 481.

29. Jill Andresky Fraser, "Women, Power and the New GE," *Working Woman*, December, 1992.

30. Gunther, "How GE Made NBC No. 1" *Fortune*, February 3, 1997.

31. Kyle Pope, "TV Networks Face Pressure to Trim Budgets," *The Wall Street Journal*, August 15, 1997.

32. Gunther, "How GE Made NBC No. 1."

33. Jack Welch, interview with author, Fairfield, CT, July 3, 1997.

34. Ibid.

35. Stratford P. Sherman, "The Mind of Jack Welch," *Fortune*, March 27, 1989, p. 39.

36. Betsy Morris, "Robert Goizueta and Jack Welch: The Wealth Builders," *Fortune*, December 11, 1995.

37. Marilyn A. Harris and Christopher Power, "He Hated Losing—Even in Touch Football," *Business Week*, June 30, 1986, p. 65.

38. Auletta, *Three Blind Mice: How the TV Networks Lost Their Way*, p. 16.

39. Jack Welch, interview with author, Fairfield, CT, July 3, 1997.

40. Morris, "Robert Goizueta and Jack Welch: The Wealth Builders."

41. Jack Welch, interview with author, Fairfield, CT, July 3, 1997.

42. Harris and Power, "He Hated Losing—Even in Touch Football,"

43. Ibid., p. 65.

44. Ikuo Hirata, "Moving toward Small-Company Soul in a Big-Company Body," *Nikkei Business*, February 21, 1994.

45. Morris, "Robert Goizueta and Jack Welch: The Wealth Builders,"

46. Ibid.

47. Jack Welch, interview with author, Fairfield, CT, July 3, 1997.

48. Ibid.

49. Ibid.

50. Ibid.

51. Morris, "Robert Goizueta and Jack Welch: The Wealth Builders,"

52. Harris and Power, "He Hated Losing—Even in Touch Football," p. 65.

53. Jack Welch, interview with author, Fairfield, CT, July 3, 1997.

54. Frank Swoboda, "Jack Welch and the Boundaryless Company," *The Washington Post*, February 27, 1994.

55. Morris, "Robert Goizueta and Jack Welch: The Wealth Builders,"

56. Auletta, *Three Blind Mice: How the TV Networks Lost Their Way*, p. 10.

57. Peter Petre, "The Man Who Brought GE to Life," *Fortune*, January 5, 1986.

58. Jack Welch, interview with author, Fairfield, CT, July 3, 1997.

59. Ibid.

60. Ibid.

61. Ibid.

62. Morris, "Robert Goizueta and Jack Welch: The Wealth Builders."

63. John F. Welch, speech at the Seventh Annual Awards Dinner of the Work in America Institute, New York, November 12, 1990.

64. Auletta, *Three Blind Mice: How the TV Networks Lost Their Way*, p. 97.

65. Jack Welch, interview with author, Fairfield, CT, July 3, 1997.

66. Jack Welch, speech at the New England Council's 1992 Private Sector New Englander of the Year Award, Boston, MA, November 11, 1992.

67. Jack Welch, interview with author, Fairfield, CT, July 3, 1997.

68. "A Conversation with Robert Goizueta and Jack Welch," *Fortune*, December 11, 1995.

69. Tom Peters and Nancy Austin, *A Passion for Excellence: The Leadership Difference* (New York: Random House, 1985), p. 138.

70. Jack Welch, interview with author, Fairfield, CT, July 3, 1997.

71. Morris, "Robert Goizueta and Jack Welch: The Wealth Builders,"

72. "Passing the Torch," *Monogram*, January-February 1981, p. 6.

73. Thomas C. Hayes, "GE Names Welch, 45, Chairman," *The New York Times*, December 20, 1980.

74. "Passing the Torch," *Monogram*, p. 6.

75. Robert Barker, "Commanding General," *Barron's*, October 15, 1984.

76. Stratford Sherman, "A Master Class in Radical Change," *Fortune*, December 13, 1993.

77. John F. Welch, speech at the National Plastics Exposition, Chicago, June 18, 1991.

78. Jack Welch, interview with author, Fairfield, CT, July 3, 1997.

79. Eric Gelman and Penelope Wang, "Jack Welch: GE's Live Wire," *Newsweek*, December 23, 1985, p. 48.

80. Charles R. Day, Jr. and Polly LaBarre, "GE: Just Your Average Everyday $60 Billion Family Grocery Store," *Industry Week*, May 2, 1994.

81. Frank Swoboda, "Jack Welch and the Boundaryless Company," *The Washington Post*, February 27, 1994.

82. Stratford P. Sherman, "The Mind of Jack Welch," *Fortune*, March 27, 1989, p. 39.

83. Tim Stevens, "Follow the Leader," *Industry Week*, November 18, 1996.

84. Charles R. Day, Jr. and Polly LaBarre, "GE: Just Your Average Everyday c60 Billion Family Grocery Store," *Industry Week*, May 2, 1994.

85. Auletta, *Three Blind Mice: How the TV Networks Lost Their Way*, p. 398.

86. Noel M. Tichy and Stratford Sherman, *Control Your Own Destiny or Someone Else Will* (New York: Currency Doubleday, 1993), p. 148.

87. Richard Tanner Pascale, *Managing on the Edge* (New York: Simon & Schuster, 1990), p. 205.

88. Tichy and Sherman, *Control Your Own Destiny or Someone Else Will*, p. 110.

89. J.P. Donlon, "Chief Executive of the Year," *Chief Executive*, July/August, 1993.

90. Peter Petre and Margaret A. Elliott, "Jack Welch: I Got a Raw Deal," *Fortune*, July 7, 1986, p. 45.

91. Jack Welch, speech to the Economic Club of Detroit, May 16, 1994.

92. "An interview with GE's Eighth Chief Executive Officer," *Monogram*, September–October 1981, p. 4.

93. Peter Petre, "The Man Who Brought GE to Life," *Fortune*, January 5, 1987, p. 76.

94. Tom Peters and Nancy Austin, *A Passion for Excellence: The Leadership Difference* (New York: Random House), 1985, p. 180.

95. Karl Weick, "Fatigue of the Spirit in Organizational Theory and Organizational Development," *Journal of Applied Behavioral Science*, September 1, 1990.

96. John F. Welch Jr., memo to Reginald Jones, Re: Success in Self-evaluation, June 2, 1980.

97. J.P. Donlon, "Chief Executive of the Year," *Chief Executive*, July/August, 1993.

98. Steven Flax, "The Toughest Boss in America," *Fortune*, August 6, 1984.

99. Jack Welch, speech to the Economic Club of Detroit, May 16, 1994.

100. Ibid.

101. Tim Smart, "GE's Welch: Fighting Like Hell to Be No. 1," *Business Week*, July 8, 1996, p. 48.

102. Jack Welch, message to shareholders, General Electric annual report, 1980.

103. John F. Welch, speech at the National Plastics Exposition, Chicago, June 18, 1991.

104. Weick, "Fatigue of the Spirit in Organizational Theory and Organizational Development."

105. Jack Welch, speech to the Economic Club of Detroit, May 16, 1994.

106. Auletta, *Three Blind Mice: How the TV Networks Lost Their Way*, p. 97.

107. Janet Guyon, "GE Chairman Welch, Though Much Praised, Starts to Draw Critics," *The Wall Street Journal*, August 4, 1988.

108. Betsy Morris, "Robert Goizueta and Jack Welch: The Wealth Builders," *Fortune*, December 11, 1995.

109. Noel M. Tichy and Stratford Sherman, *Control Your Own Destiny or Someone Else Will* (New York: Currency Doubleday, 1993), p. 82.

110. Russell Mitchell and Judith Dobrzynski, "GE's Jack Welch: How Good a Manager Is He?" *Business Week*, December 14, 1987.

111. Marilyn A. Harris, Zachary Schiller, Russell Mitchell, and Christopher Power, "Can Jack Welch Reinvent GE?" *Business Week*, June 30, 1986, p. 62.

112. Janet Guyon, "GE Chairman Welch, Though Much Praised, Starts to Draw Critics," *The Wall Street Journal*, August 4, 1988.

113. Dr. Steve Kerr, interview with author, Crotonville, NY, July 10, 1997.

114. Ibid.

115. John Curran, "GE Capital: Jack Welch's Secret Weapon," *Fortune*, November 10, 1997.

116. Richard Tanner Pascale, *Managing on the Edge* (New York: Simon & Schuster, 1990), p. 210.

117. Frank Swoboda, "Jack Welch and the Boundaryless Company," *The Washington Post*, February 27, 1994.

118. Ibid.

119. John F. Welch, speech to the National Plastics Exposition, Chicago, IL., June 18, 1991.

120. "A Troubled Star Starts Over," *Fortune*, February 3, 1997.

121. Jack Welch, General Electric annual meeting, Charlotte, NC, April 23, 1997.

122. John F. Welch, "Linkages and Leadership," address to the Commercial Club, Cincinnati, OH, October 17, 1985.

123. Stratford P. Sherman, "The Mind of Jack Welch," *Fortune*, March 27, 1989, p. 39.

124. Tichy and Sherman, *Control Your Destiny or Someone Else Will*, p. 6.

125. Jack Welch, General Electric 1997 annual meeting, Charlotte, NC, April 23, 1997.

126. Nick Turner, "Equifax Inc.'s McGlaughlin, Giving Good Directions, Then Getting Out of the Way," *Investor's Business Daily*, December 26, 1996.

127. Noel Tichy and Ram Charan, "Speed, Simplicity and Self-Confidence: An Interview with Jack Welch," *Harvard Business Review*, September–October, 1989, p. 112.

128. R. Corelli and V. Dwyer, "Jack Welch Reinvents General Electric—Again," *The Economist*, March 3, 1991, p. 59.

129. Peter Petre, "The Man Who Brought GE to Life," *Fortune*, January 5, 1987, p. 76.

130. Jack Welch, interview with author, Fairfield, CT, July 3, 1997.

131. Marshall Loeb, "Jack Welch Lets Fly on Budgets, Bonuses, and Buddy Boards," *Fortune*, May 29, 1996.

132. Charles R. Day, Jr. and Polly LaBarre, "GE: Just Your Average Everyday $60 Billion Family Grocery Store," *Industry Week*, May 2, 1994.

133. Jack Welch, speech to shareholders, General Electric annual meeting, Greenville, SC, April 26, 1989.

134. Jack Welch, speech at the 50th Anniversary annual meeting of the North Carolina Citizens for Business and Industry, Raleigh, NC, March 18, 1992.

135. Jack Welch, speech to the Economic Club of Detroit, May 16, 1994.

136. Ibid.

137. Jack Welch, speech at the 50th Anniversary annual meeting of the North Carolina Citizens for Business and Industry, Raleigh, NC, March 18, 1992.

138. Loeb, "Jack Welch Lets Fly on Budgets, Bonuses, and Buddy Boards."

139. Day, Jr. and LaBarre, "GE: Just Your Average Everyday $60 Billion Family Grocery Store," *Industry Week*, May 2, 1994.

140. Jack Welch, speech to shareholders, General Electric annual meeting, Waukesha, WI, April 27, 1988.

141. Day, Jr. and LaBarre, "GE: Just Your Average Everyday $60 Billion Family Grocery Store."

142. Richard Tanner Pascale, *Managing on the Edge* (New York: Simon & Schuster, 1990), p.192.

143. Stratford P. Sherman, "The Mind of Jack Welch," *Fortune*, March 27, 1989, p.39.

144. Jack Welch, speech at the New England Council's 1992 Private Sector New Englander of the Year Award, Boston, MA, November 11, 1992.

145. John F. Welch, "Growing Fast in a Slow-Growth Economy," speech to financial community representatives, Hotel Pierre, New York City, December 8, 1981.

146. Tichy and Sherman, *Control Your Own Destiny or Someone Else Will*, p. 71.

147. Ibid., p 159

148. Dr. Steve Kerr, interview with Janet Lowe, Crotonville, NY, July 10, 1997.

149. Ibid.

150. Ibid.

151. Ibid.

152. John F. Welch, GE annual letter to shareholders, 1996 annual report.

153. Linda Grant, "GE's Smart Bomb Strategy," *Fortune*, July 21, 1997, p. 109.

154. Noel Tichy and Ram Charan, "Speed, Simplicity, Self-Confidence: An Interview with Jack Welch," *Harvard Business Review*, September–October, 1989, p. 112.

155. "Jack Welch: 'I Got a Raw Deal,'" *Fortune*, July 7, 1986.

156. Mike Boyer, "Wrongful-Firing Lawsuit Will Offer Look Inside GE," *Gannett News Service*, February 10, 1994.

157. William M. Carley, "The Whistle-Blower's Bug," *The Wall Street Journal*, December 28, 1994.

158. Ibid.

159. David Warshaw, "Sharing at Every Level," *Monogram*, Fall 1988.

160. Jack Welch, interview with author, Fairfield, CT, July 3, 1997.

161. Tichy and Sherman, *Control Your Own Destiny or Someone Else Will*, p. 111.

216

162. "The Spirit and the Letter of Our Commitment," General Electric, Fairfield, CT, 1993.

163. "General Electric: The Financial Wizards Switch Back to Technology," *Business Week*, March 16, 1981, p. 110.

164. Jack Welch, comments to GE corporate officer, Crotonville, NY, February 2, 1987.

165. John F. Welch, General Electric 1992 annual report, message to shareholders.

166. Frank Swoboda, "Jack Welch and the Boundaryless Company," *The Washington Post*, February 27, 1994.

167. Bill Lane, "Liberating GE's Energy," *Monogram*, Fall 1989, p. 3.

168. Russell Mitchell and Judith Dobrzynski, "GE's Jack Welch: How Good a Manager Is He?" *Business Week*, December 14, 1987.

169. Richard Tanner Pascale, *Managing on the Edge* (New York: Simon & Schuster, 1990), p. 205.

170. Jack Welch, speech to shareholders, General Electric annual meeting, Waukesha, WI, April 27, 1988.

171. Frank Swoboda, "Talking Management with Chairman Welch," *The Washington Post*, March 23, 1997.

172. Tichy and Sherman, *Control Your Own Destiny or Someone Else Will*, p. 212.

173. Charles R. Day, Jr. and Polly LaBarre, "GE: Just Your Average Everyday $60 Billion Family Grocery Store," *Industry Week*, May 2, 1994.

174. Bill Lane, "Liberating GE's Energy," *Monogram*, Fall 1989,

175. Tichy and Sherman, *Control Your Own Destiny or Someone Else Will*, p. 10.

176. John F. Welch, "Growing Fast in a Slow-Growth Economy," speech to financial community representatives, Hotel Pierre, New York City, December 8, 1981.

177. Jack Welch, speech to the 50th Anniversary annual meeting of the North Carolina Citizens for Business and Industry, Raleigh, NC, March 18, 1992.

178. Jack Welch, speech to New York University's Stern School of Business, as reported by Marshall Loeb, *Fortune*, May 29, 1996.

179. General Electric, letter to shareholders, February 9, 1996, p. 2.

180. "An interview with GE's Eighth Chief Executive Officer," *Monogram*, September–October, 1981, p. 4.

181. Tim Smart and Judith H. Dobrzynski, "Jack Welch on the Art of Thinking Small," *Business Week*, Enterprise 1993, p. 212

182. General Electric, letter to shareholders, February 9, 1996, p. 2.

183. Jack Welch, speech to shareholders, General Electric 1993 annual meeting, Fort Wayne, IN, April 28, 1992.

184. Tim Smart and Judith H. Dobrzynski, "Jack Welch on the Art of Thinking Small," *Business Week*, Enterprise 1993, p. 212.

185. Jack Welch, speech at the Seventh Annual Awards Dinner of the Work in America Institute, New York, November 13, 1990.

186. Thomas A. Stewart, "GE Keeps Those Ideas Coming," *Fortune*, August 12, 1991, pp. 41–49.

187. Tichy and Sherman, *Control Your Own Destiny or Someone Else Will*, p. 73.

188. Jack Welch, interview with author, Fairfield, CT, July 3, 1997.

189. J.F. Welch, speech to the Bay Area Council, San Francisco, CA, July 6, 1989.

190. Russell Mitchell and Judith Dobrzynski, "GE's Jack Welch: How Good a Manager Is He?" *Business Week*, December 14, 1987.

191. Tichy and Sherman, *Control Your Own Destiny or Someone Else Will*, p. 246.

192. Peter Petre, "What Welch Has Wrought at GE," *Fortune*, July 7, 1986, p. 43.

193. Egon Zehnder International, "Focus: Value Management," January 1997.

194. Ikuo Hirata, "The Past Is an Impediment in Changing Times," *Nikkei Business*, November 18, 1996.

195. Jack Welch, GE Management Conference, October 1981.

196. Jack Welch, interview with author, Fairfield, CT, July 3, 1997.

197. Richard Tanner Pascale, *Managing on the Edge* (New York: Simon & Schuster, 1990), p. 204.

198. Jack Welch, speech to shareholders, General Electric annual meeting, Fort Wayne, IN, April 28, 1993.

199. Tichy and Sherman, *Control Your Own Destiny or Someone Else Will*, p. 139.

200. David Warshaw, "An Interview with Jack Welch," *Monogram*, Fall, 1984, p. 10.

201. Jack Welch, speech to shareholders, General Electric annual meeting, Erie, PA, April 25, 1990.

202. Jack Welch, speech to shareholders, General Electric annual meeting, Waukesha, WI, April 27, 1988.

203. "CEO of the Year," *Financial World*, April 3, 1990, cover.

204. David Warshaw, "Sharing at Every Level," *Monogram*, Fall 1988.

205. Jack Welch, General Electric 1987 annual report, message to shareholders.

206. Peter Petre, "What Welch Has Wrought at GE," *Fortune*, July 7, 1986.

207. Egon Zehnder International, "Focus: Value Management," January 1997.

208. John F. Welch, Jr., "Shun the Incremental: Go for the Quantum Leap," Hatfield Fellow Lecture at Cornell University, reprinted in *Financier*, July 1984.

209. Jack Welch, speech to operations managers meeting, Boca Raton, January 1987.

210. Tichy and Sherman, *Control Your Own Destiny or Someone Else Will*, p.83.

211. Ibid.

218

212. Marilyn A. Harris, Zachary Schiller, Russell Mitchell, and Christopher Power, "Can Jack Welch Reinvent GE?" *Business Week*, June 30, 1986, p. 62.

213. Richard Tanner Pascale, *Managing on the Edge* (New York: Simon & Schuster, 1990), p. 211.

214. GE home page, Overview, Leadership & Training, www.ge.com

215. Tichy and Sherman, *Control Your Own Destiny or Someone Else Will*, p. 246.

216. Tim Stevens, "Follow the Leader," *Industry Week*, November 18, 1996.

217. Stratford Sherman, "A Master Class in Radical Change," *Fortune*, December 13, 1993.

218. Egon Zehnder International, "Focus: Value Management," January 1997.

219. Jack Welch, speech to the 50th Anniversary annual meeting of the North Carolina Citizens for Business and Industry, Raleigh, NC, March 18, 1992.

220. "Unions: A Blast from Neutron Jack," *Business Week*, March 24, 1997, p. 178.

221. General Electric letter to shareholders, February 9, 1996, p. 5.

222. Jack Welch, speech to the 50th Anniversary annual meeting of the North Carolina Citizens for Business and Industry, Raleigh, NC, March 18, 1992.

223. General Electric letter to shareholders, February 9, 1997, p. 5

224. Jack Welch, speech to the 50th Anniversary annual meeting of the North Carolina Citizens for Business and Industry, Raleigh, NC, March 18, 1992.

225. Ibid.

226. General Electric letter to shareholders, February 9, 1997, p. 5.

227. Jack Welch, speech to the 50th Anniversary annual meeting of the North Carolina Citizens for Business and Industry, Raleigh, NC, March 18, 1992.

228. General Electric letter to shareholders, February 9, 1997, p. 5.

229. Jack Welch, speech to the 50th Anniversary annual meeting of the North Carolina Citizens for Business and Industry, Raleigh, NC, March 18, 1992.

230. Richard Tanner Pascale, *Managing on the Edge* (New York: Simon & Schuster, 1990), p. 211.

231. Steve Kerr, interview with author, Crotonville, NY, July 10, 1997.

232. *"GE," Management Today*, May 1, 1978.

233. "An Interview with GE's Eighth Chief Executive Officer," *Monogram*, September–October 1981, p. 5.

234. John F. Welch, Jr., "Shun the Incremental: Go for the Quantum Leap," Hatfield Fellow Lecture at Cornell University, reprinted in *Financier*, July 1984.

235. Jack Welch, speech to shareholders, General Electric annual meeting, Greenville, SC, April 26, 1989.

236. Noel Tichy and Ram Charan, "Speed, Simplicity, Self-Confidence: An Interview with Jack Welch, *Harvard Business Review*, September–October, 1989, p. 112.

237. Marilyn A. Harris, Zachary Schiller, Russell Mitchell, and Christopher Power, "Can Jack Welch Reinvent GE?" *Business Week*, June 30, 1986, p. 62.

238. Dr. Steve Kerr, interview with author, Crotonville, NY, July 10, 1997.
239. Mark Potts, "GE's Management Mission," *The Washington Post*, May 22, 1988.
240. Pascale, *Managing on the Edge*, p. 204.
241. Tim Smart, "Jack Welch's Encore," *Business Week*, October 28, 1996, p. 154.
242. John F. Welch, message to shareholders, GE 1989 annual report.
243. Stratford Sherman, "A Master Class in Radical Change," *Fortune*, December 13, 1993.
244. Frank Swoboda, "Talking Management with Chairman Welch," *The Washington Post*, March 23, 1997.
245. Jack Welch, speech to the Economic Club of Detroit, May 16, 1994.
246. Jack Welch, speech to shareholders, General Electric annual meeting, Erie, PA, April 25, 1997.
247. Noel M. Tichy and Stratford Sherman, *Control Your Own Destiny or Someone Else Will* (New York: Currency Doubleday, 1993), p. 210.
248. Ibid., p. 211.
249. Dr. Steve Kerr, interview with author, Crotonville, NY, July 10, 1997.
250. John F. Welch, Jr., "Shun the Incremental: Go for the Quantum Leap," Hatfield Fellow Lecture at Cornell University, reprinted in *Financier*, July 1984.
251. Tichy and Sherman, *Control Your Own Destiny or Someone Else Will*, p. 245.
252. Jack Welch, speech, Cornell University, April 26, 1984.
253. John F. Welch, Jr., "Shun the Incremental: Go for the Quantum Leap," Hatfield Fellow Lecture at Cornell University, reprinted in *Financier*, July 1984.
254. Charles R. Day, Jr. and Polly LaBarre, "GE: Just Your Average, Everyday $60 Billion Family Grocery Store," *Industry Week*, May 2, 1994.
255. John F. Welch, Jr., "Shun the Incremental: Go for the Quantum Leap," Hatfield Fellow Lecture at Cornell University, reprinted in *Financier*, July 1984.
256. John F. Welch, address to the Commercial Club, Cincinnati, OH, October 17, 1985.
257. John F. Welch, General Electric 1985 annual report, message to shareholders.
258. Jack Welch, "A Master Class in Radical Change," *Fortune*, December 13, 1993.
259. Marshall Loeb, "Jack Welch Lets Fly on Budgets, Bonuses, and Buddy Boards," *Fortune*, May 29, 1996.
260. Jack Welch, speech to the 50th Anniversary annual meeting of the North Carolina Citizens for Business and Industry, Raleigh, NC, March 18, 1992.
261. Ibid.
262. Ibid.
263. Tichy and Sherman, *Control Your Own Destiny or Someone Else Will*, p. 76.
264. Jack Welch, speech to the Economic Club of Detroit, May 16, 1994.

265. Tichy and Sherman, *Control Your Own Destiny or Someone Else Will*, p. 167.

266. John F. Welch, letter to shareholders, GE annual report, February 11, 1994.

267. John F. Welch, speech to Bay Area Council, San Francisco, CA, July 6, 1989.

268. Jack Welch, speech at the 50th Anniversary annual meeting of the North Carolina Citizens for Business and Industry, Raleigh, NC, March 18, 1992.

269. Charles R. Day, Jr. and Polly LaBarre, "GE: Just Your Average Everyday $60 Billion Family Grocery Store," *Industry Week*, May 3, 1994.

270. Jack Welch, speech at the Economic Club of Detroit, May 16, 1994.

271. Marshall Loeb, "Jack Welch Lets Fly on Budgets, Bonuses, and Buddy Boards," *Fortune*, May 29, 1996.

272. General Electric letter to shareholders, February 10, 1995, p. 7.

273. "General Electric: The Financial Wizards Switch Back to Technology," *Business Week*, March 16, 1981, p. 110.

274. Jack Welch, speech to shareholders, General Electric annual meeting, Charlottesville, VA, April 24, 1996.

275. John F. Welch, speech to shareholders, General Electric annual meeting, Greenville, SC, April 26, 1989.

276. Ikuo Hirata, "Moving toward Small-Company Soul in a Big Company Body," *Nikkei Business*, February 21, 1994.

277. Ikuo Hirata, "The Past Is an Impediment in Changing Times," *Nikkei Business*, November 18, 1996.

278. Peter Petre and Margaret A. Elliott, "Jack Welch: I Got a Raw Deal," *Fortune*, July 7, 1986, p. 45.

279. Ken Auletta, *Three Blind Mice: How the TV Networks Lost Their Way* (New York: Random House, 1991), p. 95.

280. Jack Welch, interview with author, Fairfield, CT, July 3, 1997.

281. John F. Welch, GE 1989 annual report, message to shareholders.

282. Jack Welch, interview with author, Fairfield, CT, July 3, 1997. NOTE: Welch is frequently quoted as saying this and the quotation appears in multiple sources.

283. Ibid.

284. David Warshaw, "An Interview with Jack Welch," *Monogram*, Fall 1984, p. 11.

285. Ibid., p.12.

286. Jack Welch, interview with author, Fairfield, CT, July 3, 1997.

287. "An Interview with GE's Eighth Chief Executive Officer," *Monogram*, September–October, 1981, p. 3.

288. General Electric letter to shareholders, February 9, 1996, p. 2.

289. John F. Welch, "Growing Fast in a Slow-Growth Economy," speech to financial community representatives, Hotel Pierre, New York City, December 8, 1981.

290. Betsy Morris, "Robert Goizueta, and Jack Welch: The Wealth Builders," *Fortune*, December 11, 1995.

291. Jack Welch, speech to shareholders, General Electric annual meeting, Greenville, SC, April 26, 1989.

292. Ann M. Morrison, "Trying to Bring GE to Life," *Fortune*, January 25, 1982.

293. John F. Welch, remarks at the GE annual meeting, Greenville, SC, April 26, 1989.

294. "An Interview with GE's Eighth Chief Executive Officer," *Monogram*, September-October, 1981, p. 3.

295. Tichy and Sherman, *Control Your Own Destiny or Someone Else Will*, p. 75.

296. Ann M. Morrison, "Trying to Bring GE to Life," *Fortune*, January 25, 1982.

297. Jack Welch, speech at the 50th Anniversary annual meeting of the North Carolina Citizens for Business and Industry, Raleigh, NC, March 18, 1992.

298. Jack Welch, speech to shareholders, General Electric annual meeting, Waukesha, WI, April 27, 1988.

299. Jack Welch, speech at the New England Council's 1992 Private Sector New Englander of the Year Award, Boston, MA, November 11, 1992.

300. John F. Welch, address to shareholders, GE annual meeting, Waukesha, WI, April 27, 1988.

301. Ibid.

302. Bill Lane, "Liberating GE's Energy," *Monogram*, Fall, 1989, p. 4.

303. Stephen W. Quickel, "Welch on Welch," *Financial World*, April 3, 1990.

304. David Warshaw, "An Interview with Jack Welch," *Monogram*, Fall, 1984, p. 13.

305. Eric Gelman and Penelope Wang, "Jack Welch: GE's Live Wire," *Newsweek*, December 23, 1995, p. 48.

306. David Warshaw, "An Interview with Jack Welch," *Monogram*, Fall 1984, p. 15.

307. Ibid., p. 11.

308. Tichy and Sherman, *Control Your Own Destiny or Someone Else Will*, p. 82.

309. Jack Welch, speech to shareholders, General Electric annual meeting, Erie, PA, April 25, 1990.

310. Jack Welch, speech to shareholders, General Electric annual meeting, Waukesha, WI, April 27, 1988.

311. Jack Welch, speech to shareholders, General Electric annual meeting, Decatur, IL, April 24, 1991.

312. Jack Welch, speech at the 50th Anniversary annual meeting of the North Carolina Citizens for Business and Industry, Raleigh, NC, March 18, 1992.

313. Jack Welch, speech to shareholders, General Electric annual meeting, Fort Wayne, IN, April 28, 1993.

314. John F. Welch, GE annual report, message to shareholders, 1991.

315. Philip C. Krantz, "Letters to the Editor," *Fortune*, April 24, 1988, p. 338.

316. "An Interview with GE's Eighth Chief Executive Officer," *Monogram*, September–October 1981.

317. Jack Welch, speech at the 1989–1990 George S. Dively Award for Leadership in Corporate Public Initiative, Harvard University, Boston, MA, October 17, 1990.

318. Thomas A. Stewart, "GE Keeps Those Ideas Coming," *Fortune*, August 12, 1991, p. 41.

319. GE corporate officers meeting, Phoenix, AZ, 1983.

320. Russell Mitchell and Susan Dobrzynski, "GE's Jack Welch: How Good a Manager Is He?" *Business Week*, December 14, 1987.

321. Jack Welch, speech at the Seventh Annual Awards Dinner of the Work in America Institute, New York, NY, November 13, 1990.

322. Thomas A. Stewart, "GE Keeps Those Ideas Coming," *Fortune*, August 12, 1991, p. 41.

323. Jack Welch, "The Information Age—Finally," speech presented at the World Economic Forum, Davos, Switzerland, January 30, 1997.

324. John F. Welch, "Today's Leaders Look to Tomorrow," *Fortune*, March 26, 1990.

325. Tichy and Sherman, *Control Your Own Destiny or Someone Else Will*, p. 245.

326. Jack Welch, speech, General Electric annual meeting, Charlotte, NC, April 23, 1997.

327. Jack Welch, speech to shareholders, General Electric 1991 annual meeting, Decatur, IL, April 24, 1991.

328. Dr. Steve Kerr, interview with author, Crotonville, NY, July 10, 1997.

329. Judy Quinn, "The Welch Way," *Incentive*, September 1994.

330. Jack Welch, speech to shareholders, General Electric annual meeting, Erie, PA, April 25, 1990.

331. Egon Zehnder International, "Focus: Value Management," January 1997.

332. Jack Welch, General Electric 1994 annual report, message to shareholders.

333. Jack Welch, speech at the Seventh Annual Awards Dinner of the Work in America Institute, New York, NY, November 13, 1990.

334. Bill Lane, "Liberating GE's Energy," *Monogram*, Fall, 1989, p. 3.

335. John F. Welch, speech to shareholders, General Electric annual meeting, Greenville, SC, April 26, 1989.

336. Ibid.

337. Noel Tichy and Ram Charan, "Speed, Simplicity, Self-Confidence: An Interview with Jack Welch," *Harvard Business Review*, September–October 1989, p. 112.

338. John F. Welch, message to shareholders, General Electric 1983 annual report.

339. Distilled from GE documents and other sources.

340. John Welch, speech to shareholders, General Electric annual meeting, Waukesha, WI, April 27, 1988.

341. Bill Lane, "Liberating GE's Energy," *Monogram*, Fall 1989, p. 3.

342. Ibid.

343. Ibid., p. 2.

344. Jack Welch, speech to shareholders, General Electric 1991 annual meeting, Decatur, IL, April 24, 1991.

345. General Electric, letter to shareholders, February 10, 1995, p. 4.

346. Jack Welch, speech at the New England Council's 1992 Private Sector New Englander of the Year Award, Boston, MA, November 11, 1992.

347. General Electric letter to shareholders, February 9, 1997, p. 4.

348. Jack Welch, "The Information Age: Finally," speech presented at the World Economic Forum, Davos, Switzerland, January 30, 1997.

349. "General Electric: The Financial Wizards Switch Back to Technology," *Business Week*, March 16, 1981, p. 110.

350. Tim Smart and Judith H. Dobrzynski, "Jack Welch on the Art of Thinking Small," *Business Week*, Enterprise 1993, p. 212.

351. Jack Welch, interview with author, Fairfield, CT, July 3, 1997.

352. Jack Welch, speech to shareholders, General Electric annual meeting, Greenville, SC, April 26, 1989.

353. Peter Petre, "What Welch Has Wrought at GE," *Fortune*, July 7, 1986, p. 43.

354. Jack Welch, speech to shareholders, General Electric 1991 annual meeting, Charlottesville, VA, April 24, 1991.

355. John F. Welch, letter to shareholders, GE annual report, February 10, 1989.

356. Ibid.

357. David Warshaw, "An Interview with Jack Welch," *Monogram*, Fall 1984, p. 14.

358. Stratford Sherman, "A Master Class in Radical Change," *Fortune*, December 13, 1993.

359. Ibid.

360. Aaron Bernstein, "High Tension at General Electric," *Business Week*, March 24, 1997.

361. Ibid.

362. Ibid.

363. Jack Welch, interview with author, Fairfield, CT, July 3, 1997.

364. David Warshaw, "An Interview with Jack Welch," *Monogram*, Fall, 1984, p. 10.

365. Bill Lane, "Liberating GE's Energy," *Monogram*, Fall 1989, p. 5.

366. Jack Welch, "Today's Leaders Look to Tomorrow," *Fortune*, March 26, 1990.

367. Jack Welch, speech to shareholders, General Electric 1991 annual meeting, Decatur, IL, April 24, 1991.

368. "Create a Company of Ideas," *Fortune*, December 30, 1991.

369. Jack Welch, speech to the Economic Club of Detroit, May 16, 1994.

370. Ibid.

371. Jack Welch, General Electric annual meeting, Charlotte, NC, April 23, 1997.

372. Ibid.

373. Tim Smart, "Jack Welch's Encore," *Business Week*, October 28, 1996, p. 154.

374. Charles R. Day, Jr. and Polly LaBarre, "GE: Just Your Average Everyday $60 Billion Family Grocery Store," *Industry Week*, May 2, 1994.

375. Jill Andresky Fraser, "Women, Power, and the New GE," *Working Woman*, December 1992.

376. Jack Welch, speech to the Economic Club of Detroit, May 16, 1994.

377. John F. Welch, General Electric, letter to shareholders, February 7, 1997.

378. Ibid.

379. Jack Welch, speech to shareholders, General Electric annual meeting, Fort Wayne, IN, April 28, 1993.

380. Tim Smart and Judith H. Dobrzynski, "Jack Welch on the Art of Thinking Small," *Business Week*, Enterprise 1993, p. 212.

381. Thomas A. Stewart, "Brain Power," *Fortune*, March 17, 1997.

382. Jack Welch, General Electric, letter to shareholders, February 12, 1993.

383. John F. Welch, General Electric, letter to shareholders, February 7, 1997.

384. Jack Welch, speech to shareholders, General Electric annual meeting, Erie, PA, April 25, 1990.

385. Stephen W. Quickel, "Welch on Welch," *Financial World*, April 3, 1990.

386. Jack Welch, interview with author, Fairfield, CT, July 3, 1997.

387. Jack Welch, speech to shareholders, General Electric 1996 annual meeting, Charlottesville, VA, April 24, 1996.

388. General Electric, letter to shareholders, February 10, 1995, p. 5.

389. Jack Welch, speech to New York University's Stern School of Business, as reported by Marshall Loeb, *Fortune*, May 29, 1996.

390. John F. Welch, General Electric, letter to shareholders, February 10, 1995, p. 6.

391. Ibid.

392. Jack Welch, interview with author, Fairfield, CT, July 3, 1997.

393. John F. Welch, Jr., "Shun the Incremental: Go for the Quantum Leap," Hatfield Fellow Lecture at Cornell University, reprinted in *Financier*, July 1984.

394. John F. Welch, General Electric, letter to shareholders, February 10, 1995, p. 6.

395. Charles R. Day, Jr. and Polly LaBarre, "GE: Just Your Average Everyday $60 Billion Family Grocery Store," *Industry Week*, May 2, 1994.

396. John F. Welch, Jr., "Shun the Incremental: Go for the Quantum Leap," *Financier*, July 1984.

397. "An Interview with GE's Eighth Chief Executive Officer," *Monogram*, September–October, 1981.

398. Jack Welch, "The Information Age—Finally," speech presented to the World Economic Forum, Davos, Switzerland, January 30, 1997.

399. Jack Welch, speech to shareholders, General Electric 1996 annual meeting, Charlottesville, VA, April 24, 1996.

400. Jack Welch, interview with author, Fairfield, CT, July 3, 1997.

401. Jack Welch, General Electric 1997 annual meeting, Charlotte, NC, April 23, 1997.

402. "General Electric: The Financial Wizards Switch Back to Technology," *Business Week*, March 16, 1981, p. 110.

403. Jack Welch, speech to shareholders, General Electric 1996 annual meeting, Charlottesville, VA, April 24, 1996.

404. General Electric annual report, February 7, 1997.

405. Jack Welch, General Electric 1997 annual meeting, Charlotte, NC, April 23, 1997.

406. Jack Welch, interview with author, Fairfield, CT, July 3, 1997.

407. Jack Welch, General Electric 1997 annual meeting, Charlotte, NC, April 23, 1997.

408. John F. Welch, letter to shareholders, General Electric annual report, February 7, 1997.

409. John F. Welch, letter to shareholders, General Electric annual report, February 26, 1982.

410. David Warshaw, "An Interview with Jack Welch," *Monogram*, Fall 1984.

411. Richard Tanner Pascale, *Managing on the Edge* (New York: Simon & Schuster, 1990), p. 204.

412. Jack Welch, letter to shareholders, General Electric 1983 annual report.

413. "Technology Lets Firms Look Beyond Quality," *Investors Business Daily*, June 4, 1996.

414. John F. Welch, General Electric 1996 annual report.

415. Jack Welch, interview with author, Fairfield, CT, July 3, 1997.

416. Marilyn A. Harris, Zachary Schiller, Russell Mitchell, and Christopher Power, "Can Jack Welch Reinvent GE?" *Business Week*, June 30, 1986, p. 62.

417. "Jack Welch: 'I Got a Raw Deal,'" *Fortune*, July 7, 1986.

418. Richard Tanner Pascale, *Managing on the Edge* (New York: Simon & Schuster, 1990), p. 205.

419. David Warshaw, "An interview with Jack Welch," *Monogram*, Fall, 1984.

420. Ibid.

421. Jack Welch, interview with author, Fairfield, CT, July 3, 1997.

422. Janet Guyon, "GE Chairman Welch, Though Much Praised, Starts to Draw Critics," *The Wall Street Journal*, August 4, 1988.

423. Thomas A. Stewart, "Ideas and Solutions: The Leading Edge," *Fortune*, June 10, 1996.

424. John F. Welch, General Electric, letter to shareholders, February 10, 1995, p. 7.

425. Ibid., p. 8.

426. Betsy Morris, "Robert Goizueta and Jack Welch: The Wealth Builders," *Fortune*, December 11, 1995.

427. Jack Welch, interview with author, Fairfield, CT, July 3, 1997.

428. Noel Tichy and Stratford Sherman, *Control Your Own Destiny or Someone Else Will* (New York: Currency Doubleday, 1993), p. 91.

429. Tim Smart and Susan Chandler, "The Monkey on GE's Back," *Business Week*, May 19, 1997, p. 40.

430. Stratford Sherman, "A Master Class in Change," *Fortune*, December 13, 1993.

431. Lisa Driscoll, "The Gnat Trying to Sting an Elephant called GE," *Business Week*, June 24, 1991, p. 44.

432. Barbara Presley Noble, "Going After GE," *The New York Times*, June 16, 1991.

433. Christina Del Valle and Monica Larner, "A New Front in the War on Land Mines," *Business Week*, April 28, 1997, p. 43.

434. Janet Guyon, "GE Chairman Welch, Though Much Praised, Starts to Draw Critics," *The Wall Street Journal*, August 4, 1988.

435. Tom Peters, *In Search of Excellence* (New York: Harper Collins, 1987), as quoted in Russell Mitchell and Judith H. Dobrzynski, "GE's Jack Welch: How Good a Manager Is He?" *Business Week*, December 14, 1987.

436. Tom Peters: "Contradicting Myself 13 Ways," *Forbes* ASAP Supplement, June 6, 1994.

437. Christopher Lorenz, "Life under Jack Welch: Opportunistic and Tough," *Financial Times*, May 16, 1988.

438. Mitchell and Dobrzynski, "GE's Jack Welch: How Good a Manager Is He?"

439. Letters to *Fortune*, May 8, 1989.

440. Dr. Steven Kerr, interview with author, Crotonville, NY, July 10, 1997.

441. Guyon, "GE Chairman Welch, Though Much Praised, Starts to Draw Critics."

442. Janet Guyon, "Combative Chief: GE's Jack Welch," *The Wall Street Journal*, August 4, 1988, p. 1.

443. Letter from Grant A. Tinker to John F. Welch, January 27, 1997.

444. Paul Tharp, "Turner Mouths Off," *New York Post*, Wednesday, July 9, 1997.

445. "The Brutal Manager," *Der Spiegel*, July 14, 1997.

446. "An Interview with GE's Eighth Chief Executive Officer," *Monogram*, September–October 1981, p. 2.

447. John F. Welch, "Linkages and Leadership," address to the Commercial Club, Cincinnati, OH, October 17, 1985.

448. Ibid.

449. Jack Welch, interview with author, Fairfield, CT, July 3, 1997.

450. Michael H. Martin, "The Restaurant that Banned Jack Welch: GE-Free Dining," *Fortune*, October 14, 1996.

451. Jack Welch, interview with author, Fairfield, CT, July 3, 1997.

452. Ibid.

453. Jack Welch, speech at the 1989–90 George S. Dively Award for Leadership in Corporate Public Initiative, Harvard University, Boston, MA, October 17, 1990.

454. Ibid.

455. Ibid

456. Ibid.

457. Ibid.

458. Jack Welch, speech at the New England Council's 1992 Private Sector New Englander of the Year Award, Boston, MA, November 11, 1992.

459. John F. Welch, address to the Commercial Club, Cincinnati, OH, October 17, 1985.

460. Jack Welch, interview with author, Fairfield, CT, July 3, 1997.

461. Michael Connor, "GE CEO defines $28.2 Million Paycheck," *Reuters Business Report*, April 23, 1997.

462. Ikuo Hirata, "The Past Is an Impediment in a Changing World," *Nikkei Business*, November 18, 1996.

463. Andrew Bary, "GE Is a Powerhouse in the S&P 500, But a Relative Weakling in Some Portfolios," *Barron's*, May 19, 1997, p. MW3.

464. Allan Sloan, "How Much Is Too Much?" *Newsweek*, March 17, 1997.

465. Frank Swoboda, "Talking Management with Chairman Welch," *The Washington Post*, March 23, 1997.

466. Joyce Hergenhan, interview with author, Fairfield, CT, July 3, 1997.

467. Linda Grant, "GE: The Envelope Please," *Fortune*, June 26, 1995.

468. Marc Nexon, "The Secrets of the Finest Company in the World," *L'Expansion*, July 10–24, 1997.

469. Linda Grant, "GE: The Envelope Please," *Fortune*, June 26, 1995.

470. Dr. Steve Kerr, interview with author, Crotonville, NY, July 10, 1997.

471. Jack Welch, interview with author, Fairfield, CT, July 3, 1997.

472. Ibid.

473. Grant, "GE: The Envelope Please."

474. Thomas A. Stewart, "GE Keeps Those Ideas Coming," *Fortune*, August 12, 1991, p. 41.

475. Jack Welch, interview with Janet Lowe, Fairfield, CT, July 3, 1997.

476. "We're Driven by Soft Values," *Business Today*, February 7–21, 1995.

477. Dr. Steve Kerr, interview with author, Crotonville, NY, July 10, 1997.

478. Jennifer Reingold, "Where Parting Is Such a Sweet Deal," *Business Week*, March 31, 1997.

479. Steve Kerr, interview with author, Crotonville, NY, July 10, 1997.

480. Jack Welch, speech at the New England Council's 1992 Private Sector New Englander of the Year Award, Boston, MA, November 11, 1992.

481. Noel M. Tichy and Stratford Sherman, *Control Your Own Destiny or Someone Else Will* (New York: Currency Doubleday, 1993), p. 210.
482. Jack Welch, interview with author, Fairfield, CT, July 3, 1997.
483. Ibid.
484. Ibid.
485. Ibid.
486. Marc Nexon, "The Secrets of the Finest Company in the World," *L'Expansion*, July 10, 1997.

PERMISSIONS

Permission has been granted by the following organizations for quotes appearing in this book:

Business Week

Chief Executive

Der Spiegel

Control Your Destiny or Someone Else Will by Noel M. Tichy and Stratford Sherman. Copyright ©1993 by Noel M. Tichy and Stratford Sherman. Used by permission of Doubleday, a division of Bantam Doubleday Dell Publishing Group, Inc.

Financial Times

Fortune

Reprinted by permission of *Harvard Business Review*. Excerpt from "Speed, Simplicity and Self Confidence: An Interview with Jack Welch" by Noel M. Tichy and Ram Charan, September–October, 1989. Copyright 1989 by the President and Fellows of Harvard College; all rights reserved.

Incentive

Reprinted with permission from *IndustryWeek*. Excerpt from "GE, Just Your Average Everyday $60 Billion Family Grocer Store" by Charles R. Ray, Jr. and Polly LaBarre, May 2, 1994. Copyright, Penton Publishing, Inc., Cleveland, Ohio.

Investor's Business Daily

Karl Weick, "Fatigue of the Spirit in Organizational Theory and Organizational Development," *Journal of Applied Behavioral Science*, September 1, 1990.

From *Newsweek*, "Jack Welch: GE's Live Wire," by Eric Gelman and Penelope Wang, © 1985, Newsweek, Inc. All rights reserved. Reprinted by permission.

Nikkei Business

From *Three Blind Mice* by Ken Auletta. Copyright © 1991 by Ken Auletta. Reprinted by permission of Random House, Inc., and International Creative Management, Inc.

Reprinted by permission of Simon & Schuster from *Managing on the Edge* by Richard Tanner Pascale. Copyright © 1990 by Richard Pascale.

Excerpts reprinted by permission of *The Wall Street Journal*, © 1988 Dow Jones & Company, Inc. All rights reserved worldwide.

The Washington Post

SOUTHEASTERN COMMUNITY COLLEGE LIBRARY

3 3255 00069 7731

HD 9697 .A3 U585 1998

Lowe, janet C.
Jack Welch speaks

SOUTHEASTERN COMMUNITY
    COLLEGE LIBRARY
WHITEVILLE, NC 28472